JOURNAL YOUR WAY TO SUCCESS

by Sandie Troup

INTRODUCTION

Welcome to your journey on organizing your day with intention, no more flying by the seat of your pants hoping the day works out. The goal with this journal is to organize your life and finally fit in all those activities you struggle to find time to do during your busy work week. So fasten your seat belt and get ready to tackle life with ease and feel more energy and endurance. I have learned that my commitment to these activities in this journal have allowed me to experience more success at work, in my personal life and I have more peace and balance throughout my day! My hope is that if you too can commit some time to these activities included in this journal that you may also experience changes in your life, so let's make the next 3 months the best 3 months of your life.

The prescription for your success is that you enter into this program with an open mind and the willingness to try new and different things. You will engage in activities for 12 weeks, journaling your results and thoughts and I will challenge you as the weeks progress. My hope is at the end of 3 months you are happier, stronger physically and seeing the fruit of your success in your career.

For some, initially this may be easy and for others this may feel daunting and unreasonable. But practice is the key. I have found there is power in writing down your goals, so put away your phone for one hour and you may find by journaling results, you are more clear and ready for the day and achieving goals you never thought you would attain. The key to making this work for you, is to set aside one hour per day, I recommend this be in the morning as this is when most of us are thinking more clearly and have more time. I know, you may need to set your alarm for one hour earlier, but it may be worth it! Or maybe you are at your best in the afternoon or evening, you are the expert on you, you decide. For me, morning is more predictable, I know I can make time at 5am as I find most of my days can get hijacked and then I tend to sacrifice my self-care time. Be mindful with how you schedule this time and be ready to commit.

Try it, trust me, it works. I am NOT a morning person and this was a challenge. Yet, I found myself excited to wake up each day and tackle my next day with excitement rather than dread, I found this new energy I thought I never had.

I have learned that taking care of myself is not only empowering, it allows me to be more successful in my career and it also seeped into my personal life! When I started my day feeling more refreshed and organized, I was able to take that to work and to my family and friends. There is power in feeding your soul! My business relationships and my personal relationships were more fulfilling too -- all because I found one hour in my day to do the activities in this journal.

This journal will guide you to start your day with some self-care that is life changing. I have learned you have to take care of you before you can take care of your job and others. You cannot be present at work or for your family if you haven't taken care of yourself first. Most people these days are running on empty and don't have the strength or energy to do a good job in their career, spend quality time with friends or cultivate their marriage.

This lack of self-care can create a feeling of low energy, lack of confidence, lack of control or organization in your day, issues at work or struggles at home. Let's face it you can't take care of anything in your life, if you aren't taking care of you! This is similar to when you board an airplane and you hear the lifesaving instructions, when they say, "In the event of an emergency, put your oxygen mask on FIRST and then assist your child." Even airlines tell you, help yourself first and then your child.

I challenge you to step out of your comfort zone and you too may find that new energy and control in your life. I realize some of you may have never thought about starting your day with a quiet time, you may think it's a bit silly or unnecessary. Just give it a whirl for one week. You may change your mind. Or if you don't like to exercise, or you actually despise it, then you can choose to just move your body every day, the key here being just be mindful about moving your body. You can walk up and down your stairs for the amount of time recommended, take the dog on an extra-long walk, play chase with the kids in the living room for 10 minutes, or whatever else you would like to do, just move. Trust me, you will feel better, and your dog or kids may love you more for the time they get to be with you! It's a win, win.

I am merely making recommendations on what to do. You get the chance to ultimately decide, just let this journal be your guide and through your notes you may eventually see on paper your progress and successes! You may decide not to do all the activities and that's okay. Or maybe doing these activities at night is best for you, that's okay too. You should find what works for you and what feels good.

I found this process to be so enlightening and powerful! So get ready to feel better and be prepared to answer questions from those around you, when they notice your newfound change. Co-workers may notice your increased sales; your boss may see all the projects you completed; or you may just hear, "You look great. Have you lost weight? You look so calm and happy; I want what you have!"

This journal is broken down into specific activities and as you move through the weeks, the activities will grow and change, just as you will grow and change personally and professionally. I challenge you to embrace this journal and see how you can journal your way to success!

You will experience each week the following activities:

QUIET TIME

Activity Number One. Finding 10 mins in your morning to be quiet, still your mind and control your stress. Life these days is more stressful than ever. Statistics show there are more people taking antidepressants or addicted to alcohol or drugs to cope with the chaos in life. Life for younger generations is one filled with terrorist attacks or mass shootings in malls, movie theaters and schools, this unsafe feeling can be paralyzing. Our jobs are more demanding than ever, now you are expected to answer that text, Yammer message, skype call or email outside of work hours and the unreasonable expectations of your career can cause undue stress that then goes home to your family and friends. So how do we manage that anxiety and stress? A quiet time. I know this seems way too simple but learning to quiet and calm yourself can carry you all day long. You may even find in extreme stress, you may need to find some private space to take a moment and be still. Studies show that taking a few minutes to breath, connect spiritually with yourself or meditating can relieve a majority of our stress. Now I know how I first responded to this and I can imagine you are thinking the same, this is silly. But trust me, wouldn't it be a relief to not need those pills and just chose to breathe instead? Be open minded, you may be surprised.

GOAL SETTING

Activity Number Two. Goal setting can be what you want it to be. You can set goals for the day, maybe you want to complete that report at work or maybe it will be to clean out the closet and donate some clothes. Or maybe you want to set some longer-term goals, something you want to achieve in the next month, 6 months or a year. Maybe you want to set your sights on that promotion at work or running that marathon for the first time. You can pick your goals! Not a goal setter? That's okay, then dream, I have heard a saying that, "a goal is a dream with an end date", I love that. Maybe you want to note some dreams, maybe you are dreaming of finding a new job in the next year, or you dream of taking that vacation to Europe or Lake Tahoe, dream away! I have learned that by setting an intentional goal or dream and repeating that daily, I find the strength and focus to achieve that goal or dream. I have learned that I can achieve almost anything when I set my mind to do so, so let me help guide you to find your inner power and strength to make your goals a reality!

GRATITIDE LIST

Studies show that when we focus on what we are grateful for we have a more positive attitude and that can carry us through our entire day. I use to be fairly negative but I focused on the negative, I was focusing on what wasn't working, what was stressing me out, I focused on the bad weather rather than counting my blessings. I realize when I take the time and write down all the good things in my life, I then focus on the positive and I feel more uplifted and light most of the day. I am happier when I focus on the great things in my life, like my children, the sunset, my yummy cup of morning coffee (I love coffee!), my great hair or how snuggly and cute my dog is. Count your blessings and you may see you are living a good life and as this journey continues that life may even get better!

MORNING WORKOUT

Most think they have to work out for one hour, sweat like a crazy person and go to a gym, that's not true. No one size fits all. We are all different and we like different ways to move our bodies. The key here is to move your body. Again, we all hear about how exercise helps us maintain a reasonable weight, prevent disease and significantly can reduce stress and anxiety. Plus, you may even find its fun, yes, you read that right, it can be fun! Working out can mean playing with the kiddos, walking that cute, snuggly dog or kicking butt at the gym, you pick, it's your body. I will challenge you more and more as we move into the latter weeks so get ready to get in shape, feel better, find more endurance at work and maybe fit in those tight jeans. Maybe that's one of your goals? Be open minded and you may have fun and get into shape, but remember you don't have to do everything. Ease into the activities and if you are feeling overwhelmed, always listen to your body and adjust your exercise accordingly.

MORNING MEAL

We all hear about how important this first meal of the day is, breakfast, actually we are breaking the fast that are body experienced while we slept. I believe the key to starting your day right is to choose to put some good, healthy, nutritious food into your body. I will admit, I am keen on eating healthy ALL day but it's all about baby steps with life transitions, if eating breakfast or even eating healthy is new for you, you can choose to make small adjustments, even small changes can make a big difference. I discovered that not only I felt better but I looked better, my skin was brighter and clearer, my hair wasn't as dry and I found a key to losing and maintaining my weight. I discovered that starting with one healthy meal made me crave a healthy lunch and dinner too and I wanted my family to experience the same thing so I started preparing healthier meals. I challenge you to do some research, food in the US is tricky, organic is not always organic, "healthy" doesn't really mean healthy, there are GMOs, gluten and all kinds of crazy crap in our food that is labeled and packaged to look like it is healthy for us. Can you tell this is a trigger for me? I go nuts with how much people underestimate a healthy diet. I am around so many wonderful people that experience serious diseases like heart disease, diabetes and cancers and many of these diseases can simply be prevented with a healthy diet. Restaurants have even figured it out, there are so many amazing healthy choices so even eating out can be healthy and enjoyable! The key here is to make small adjustments, maybe you start with the first meal of the day and replace one unhealthy food with a healthy food. Start with baby steps, every little bit helps!

IMPORTANT THINGS TO DO TODAY

We all have daily appointments and responsibilities, that's life! Use this space to list the appointments you have that day and details about those appointments. This may be doctors' appointments, meetings or social events. You may note the time and location and anything pertinent to that event. Maybe you have a doctor's appointment and you need to note what you need to tell your doctor about what physical pains you may be experiencing, how many of us forget to mention that weird pain in our back that shows up after we eat, or maybe you have an interview that day, so this section allows you the space to think ahead and note key questions you may want to ask the recruiter or hiring manager. Note a key meeting for that day, list tasks you may want to achieve in that meeting or maybe you have an appointment with your therapist, you can note the time and the conflicts or issues you want to address with her/him. Remember this is your journal, use this space as you see fit, you may not have anything or you may find this is just a great reminder to change that hair appointment or call that one special friend to meet for lunch, use it as a to-do list. I have found that sometimes putting those items or thoughts on paper, my head stops swirling, and it helps me feel less stressed and more peaceful during the day. I find that being thoughtful about tasks in the beginning of the day, when you are rested, may result in a more successful day!

WEEK ONE
DAY ONE

Date _____

Quiet Time (10mins) Chose 1 activity or find your own.

Practice Breathing: Take 5 deep breaths, breathing in deeply, breathing out deeply. Listen to your breath and tune into your body and listen to how amazing it is!

Listen to a Meditation App: There are lots of categories and choices, check them out.

Read some inspiring quotes from your favorite book or find someone to follow on Instagram that focuses on inspirational topics.

My own meditation activity today was, track any thoughts:

_____

_____

Goal Setting (10 mins) Personal or professional goals.

What do you need to achieve today, keep it simple. These are your personal or professional goals that you are confident you can do if you put your mind to it. Goals can look like this: Be more patient with the cashier at the coffee house, complete that report that I have been pushing aside for 3 weeks, paint more daughter's toenails, or find a new job and apply for 5 jobs today and try to find a phone number of a hiring manager or recruiter working for the firm I am interested in being hired at. Writing this down helps you to be more intentional!

_____

_____

Gratitude List (10 mins) Studies show that when you take just a few minutes to jot down those things in your life you are thankful for, you can recognize all the good in your life. Stop focusing on what's not working and start to see what is amazing in your life. This can look like: My morning coffee, sunsets, my kids hugging my leg, their giggles as they eat breakfast, my job and my salary, I can pay my bills, my family. You get the picture.

_____

_____

Morning Workout (20mins) Chose 1 activity or find your own.

Take a walk, walk the dog, walk up and down my stairs.

Get a yoga app and find some space in your family room or most yoga studios offer your first class for free, check one out in your area.

Gym workout for you gym-rats or try a class at your gym.

Track your workout, time you spent and what you did.

_____

_____

Morning Meal (10mins) The most important meal of the day! No more muffins, doughnuts, or sugar filled cereals or eating nothing. Focus on healthy choices, like protein, fruit, and simple carbohydrates if you need that. Here are some choices or find some of your own. Just making one change to your breakfast, by replacing one item in your meal with a healthy one is a good start! And don't forget to drink water, lots of water, ½ your body weight in ounces, so if you weigh 120 you need 60 ounces of water per day!

Protein shake: Find one with 20 grams of protein and watch the sugar. Load her up, add coconut or almond milk instead of milk, add fruit (i.e.: banana, blueberry) or maybe some greens (i.e.: spinach, kale). This could be your nutrition filled meal that gets you going!

3-4 Egg Whites, with onion, spinach or just plain, some blueberries and piece of toast (I personally don't like gluten) but your choice. There some good gluten free breads -give them a try, remember be open-minded!

Protein bar: Make sure it has 20 grams of protein and watch the fat and sugar. I personally like Quest, Cliff, or Kind bars. One piece of fruit or handful of blueberries.

Oatmeal: Try adding almond or coconut milk instead of milk, or don't add sugar. Add blueberries instead, or better yet, find a gluten-free oatmeal with almond milk, honey, and some almonds

Yum! Track what you ate and how you feel.

_____

_____

Important Things to Do Today

This may be a list of the key appointments today, Dr. Appt., interview, note times and key questions you don't want to forget about, etc.

_____

_____

WEEK ONE
DAY TWO

Date _____

Quiet Time (10mins) Chose 1 activity or find your own.

Practice Breathing: Take 5 deep breaths, breathing in deeply, breathing out deeply. Listen to your breath and tune into your body and how amazing it is!

Listen to a Meditation App: There are lots of categories and choices, check them out.

Read some inspiring quotes from your favorite book or find someone to follow on Instagram that focuses on inspirational topics.

My own meditation activity today was, track any thoughts:

_____

_____

Goal Setting (10 mins) Personal or professional goals.

What do you need to achieve today, keep it simple. These are your personal or professional goals that you are confident you can do if you put your mind to it. Goals can look like this: Be more patient with the cashier at the coffee house, complete that report that I have been pushing aside for 3 weeks, paint more daughter's toenails, or apply for 5 jobs today and try to find a phone number of a hiring manager or recruiter working for the firm I am interested in being hired at. Writing this down helps you to be more intentional!

_____

_____

Gratitude List (10 mins) Studies show that when you take just a few minutes to jot down those things in your life you are thankful for, you can recognize all the good in your life. Stop focusing on what's not working and start to see what is amazing in your life. This can look like: My morning coffee, sunsets, my kids hugging my leg, their giggles as they eat breakfast, my job and my salary, I can pay my bills, my family. You get the picture.

_____

_____

15

Morning Workout (20mins) Chose 1 activity or find your own.

Take a walk, walk the dog, walk up and down my stairs.

Get a yoga app and find some space in your family room or most yoga studios offer your first class for free, check one out in your area.

Gym workout for you gym-rats or try a class at your gym.

Track your workout, time you spent and what you did.

Morning Meal (10mins) The most important meal of the day! No more muffins, doughnuts, or sugar filled cereals or eating nothing. Focus on healthy choices, like protein, fruit, and simple carbohydrates if you need that. Here are some choices or find some of your own. Just making one change to your breakfast, by replacing one item in your meal with a healthy one is a good start! And don't forget to drink water, lots of water, ½ your body weight in ounces, so if you weigh 120 you need 60 ounces of water per day!

Protein shake: Find one with 20 grams of protein and watch the sugar. Load her up, add coconut or almond milk instead of milk, add fruit (i.e.: banana, blueberry) or maybe some greens (i.e.: spinach, kale). This could be your nutrition filled meal that gets you going!

3-4 Egg Whites, with onion, spinach or just plain, some blueberries and piece of toast (I personally don't like gluten, but your choice. There some good gluten free breads -give them a try!

Protein bar: Make sure it has 20 grams of protein and watch the fat and sugar. I personally like Quest, Cliff, or Kind bars. One piece of fruit or handful of blueberries.

Oatmeal: Try adding almond or coconut milk instead of milk, or don't add sugar. Add blueberries instead, or better yet, find a gluten-free oatmeal with almond milk, honey, and some almonds

Yum! Track what you ate and how you feel.

Important Things to Do Today

This may be a list of the key appointments today, Dr. Appt, interview, note times, etc.

WEEK ONE
DAY THREE

Date _____

Quiet Time (10mins) Chose 1 activity or find your own.

Practice Breathing: Take 5 deep breaths, breathing in deeply, breathing out deeply. Listen to your breath and tune into your body and how amazing it is!

Listen to a Meditation App: There are lots of categories and choices, check them out.

Read some inspiring quotes from your favorite book or find someone to follow on Instagram that focuses on inspirational topics. My own meditation activity today was, track any thoughts:

_____

_____

Goal Setting (10 mins) Personal or professional goals.

What do you need to achieve today, keep it simple. These are your personal or professional goals that you are confident you can do if you put your mind to it. Goals can look like this: Be more patient with the cashier at the coffee house, complete that report that I have been pushing aside for 3 weeks, paint more daughter's toenails, or apply for 5 jobs today and try to find a phone number of a hiring manager or recruiter working for the firm I am interested in being hired at. Writing this down helps you to be more intentional!

_____

_____

Gratitude List (10 mins) Studies show that when you take just a few minutes to jot down those things in your life you are thankful for, you can recognize all the good in your life. Stop focusing on what's not working and start to see what is amazing in your life. This can look like: My morning coffee, sunsets, my kids hugging my leg, their giggles as they eat breakfast, my job and my salary, I can pay my bills, my family. You get the picture.

_____

_____

Morning Workout (20mins) Chose 1 activity or find your own.

Take a walk, walk the dog, walk up and down my stairs.

Get a yoga app and find some space in your family room or most yoga studios offer your first class for free, check one out in your area.

Gym workout for you gym-rats or try a class at your gym.

Track your workout, time you spent and what you did.

_____

_____

Morning Meal (10mins) The most important meal of the day! No more muffins, doughnuts, or sugar filled cereals or eating nothing. Focus on healthy choices, like protein, fruit, and simple carbohydrates if you need that. Here are some choices or find some of your own. Just making one change to your breakfast, by replacing one item in your meal with a healthy one is a good start! And don't forget to drink water, lots of water, ½ your body weight in ounces, so if you weigh 120 you need 60 ounces of water per day!

Protein shake: Find one with 20 grams of protein and watch the sugar. Load her up, add coconut or almond milk instead of milk, add fruit (i.e.: banana, blueberry) or maybe some greens (i.e.: spinach, kale). This could be your nutrition filled meal that gets you going!

3-4 Egg Whites, with onion, spinach or just plain, some blueberries and piece of toast (I personally don't like gluten, but your choice. There some good gluten free breads -give them a try!

Protein bar: Make sure it has 20 grams of protein and watch the fat and sugar. I personally like Quest, Cliff, or Kind bars. One piece of fruit or handful of blueberries.

Oatmeal: Try adding almond or coconut milk instead of milk, or don't add sugar. Add blueberries instead, or better yet, find a gluten-free oatmeal with almond milk, honey, and some almonds
Yum! Track what you ate and how you feel.

_____

_____

Important Things to Do Today This may be a list of the key appointments today, Dr. Appt, interview, note times, etc.

_____

_____

WEEK ONE
DAY FOUR

Date _____

Quiet Time (10mins) Chose 1 activity or find your own.

Practice Breathing: Take 5 deep breaths, breathing in deeply, breathing out deeply. Listen to your breath and tune into your body and how amazing it is!

Listen to a Meditation Ap: There are lots of categories and choices, check them out.

Read some inspiring quotes from your favorite book or find someone to follow on Instagram that focuses on inspirational topics. My own meditation activity today was, track any thoughts:

_____

_____

Goal Setting (10 mins) Personal or professional goals.

What do you need to achieve today, keep it simple. These are your personal or professional goals that you are confident you can do if you put your mind to it. Goals can look like this: Be more patient with the cashier at the coffee house, complete that report that I have been pushing aside for 3 weeks, paint more daughter's toenails, or apply for 5 jobs today and try to find a phone number of a hiring manager or recruiter working for the firm I am interested in being hired at. Writing this down helps you to be more intentional!

_____

_____

Gratitude List (10 mins) Studies show that when you take just a few minutes to jot down those things in your life you are thankful for, you can recognize all the good in your life. Stop focusing on what's not working and start to see what is amazing in your life. This can look like: My morning coffee, sunsets, my kids hugging my leg, their giggles as they eat breakfast, my job and my salary, I can pay my bills, my family. You get the picture.

_____

_____

Morning Workout (20mins) Chose 1 activity or find your own.

Take a walk, walk the dog, walk up and down my stairs.

Get a yoga ap and find some space in your family room or most yoga studios offer your first class for free, check one out in your area.

Gym workout for you gym-rats or try a class at your gym.

Track your workout, time you spent and what you did.

_____

_____

Morning Meal (10mins) The most important meal of the day! No more muffins, doughnuts, or sugar filled cereals or eating nothing. Focus on healthy choices, like protein, fruit, and simple carbohydrates if you need that. Here are some choices or find some of your own. Just making one change to your breakfast, by replacing one item in your meal with a healthy one is a good start! And don't forget to drink water, lots of water, ½ your body weight in ounces, so if you weigh 120 you need 60 ounces of water per day!

Protein shake: Find one with 20 grams of protein and watch the sugar. Load her up, add coconut or almond milk instead of milk, add fruit (i.e.: banana, blueberry) or maybe some greens (i.e.: spinach, kale). This could be your nutrition filled meal that gets you going!

3-4 Egg Whites, with onion, spinach or just plain, some blueberries and piece of toast (I personally don't like gluten, but your choice. There some good gluten free breads -give them a try!

Protein bar: Make sure it has 20 grams of protein and watch the fat and sugar. I personally like Quest, Cliff, or Kind bars. One piece of fruit or handful of blueberries.

Oatmeal: Try adding almond or coconut milk instead of milk, or don't add sugar. Add blueberries instead, or better yet, find a gluten-free oatmeal with almond milk, honey, and some almonds

Yum! Track what you ate and how you feel.

_____

_____

WEEK ONE
DAY FIVE

Date _____

Quiet Time (10mins) Chose 1 activity or find your own.

Practice Breathing: Take 5 deep breaths, breathing in deeply, breathing out deeply. Listen to your breath and tune into your body and how amazing it is!

Listen to a Meditation App: There are lots of categories and choices, check them out.

Read some inspiring quotes from your favorite book or find someone to follow on Instagram that focuses on inspirational topics. My own meditation activity today was, track any thoughts:

_____

_____

Goal Setting (10 mins) Personal or professional goals.

What do you need to achieve today, keep it simple. These are your personal or professional goals that you are confident you can do if you put your mind to it. Goals can look like this: Be more patient with the cashier at the coffee house, complete that report that I have been pushing aside for 3 weeks, paint more daughter's toenails, or apply for 5 jobs today and try to find a phone number of a hiring manager or recruiter working for the firm I am interested in being hired at. Writing this down helps you to be more intentional!

_____

_____

Gratitude List (10 mins) Studies show that when you take just a few minutes to jot down those things in your life you are thankful for, you can recognize all the good in your life. Stop focusing on what's not working and start to see what is amazing in your life. This can look like: My morning coffee, sunsets, my kids hugging my leg, their giggles as they eat breakfast, my job and my salary, I can pay my bills, my family. You get the picture.

_____

_____

Morning Workout (20mins) Chose 1 activity or find your own.

Take a walk, walk the dog, walk up and down my stairs.

Get a yoga app and find some space in your family room or most yoga studios offer your first class for free, check one out in your area.

Gym workout for you gym-rats or try a class at your gym.

Track your workout, time you spent and what you did.

_____

_____

Morning Meal (10mins) The most important meal of the day! No more muffins, doughnuts, or sugar filled cereals or eating nothing. Focus on healthy choices, like protein, fruit, and simple carbohydrates if you need that. Here are some choices or find some of your own. Just making one change to your breakfast, by replacing one item in your meal with a healthy one is a good start! And don't forget to drink water, lots of water, ½ your body weight in ounces, so if you weigh 120 you need 60 ounces of water per day!

Protein shake: Find one with 20 grams of protein and watch the sugar. Load her up, add coconut or almond milk instead of milk, add fruit (i.e.: banana, blueberry) or maybe some greens (i.e.: spinach, kale). This could be your nutrition filled meal that gets you going!

3-4 Egg Whites, with onion, spinach or just plain, some blueberries and piece of toast (I personally don't like gluten, but your choice. There some good gluten free breads -give them a try!

Protein bar: Make sure it has 20 grams of protein and watch the fat and sugar. I personally like Quest, Cliff, or Kind bars. One piece of fruit or handful of blueberries.

Oatmeal: Try adding almond or coconut milk instead of milk, or don't add sugar. Add blueberries instead, or better yet, find a gluten-free oatmeal with almond milk, honey, and some almonds

Yum! Track what you ate and how you feel.

_____

_____

Important Things to Do Today

This may be a list of the key appointments today, Dr. Appt, interview, note times, etc.

_____

_____

WEEK TWO
DAY ONE

Date _____

Quiet Time (10mins) Chose 1 activity or find your own.

Practice Breathing: Take 5 deep breaths, breathing in deeply, breathing out deeply. Listen to your breath and tune into your body and how amazing it is!

Listen to a Meditation App.

Read some inspiring quotes from your favorite book or find someone to follow on Instagram that focuses on inspirational topics.

My own meditation activity today was, track any thoughts:

_____

_____

Goal Setting (10 mins) Personal or professional goals.

What do you need to achieve today, keep it simple. These are your personal or professional goals that you are confident you can do if you put your mind to it. Goals can look like this: In the next year, open a coffee shop, be promoted in the next 3 months to the next level in my firm or clean out that closet in the kids room by the end of the week Writing this down helps you to be more intentional and focused!

_____

_____

Gratitude List (10 mins) Stop focusing on what's not working and start to see what is amazing in your life. This can look like: My morning coffee, sunrises, my kids, or that wonderful friend.

_____

_____

Morning Workout (20mins) Chose 1 activity or find your own.

    Take a walk, walk the dog, walk up and down my stairs.

    Get a yoga app and find some space in your family room or most yoga studios offer your first class for free, check one out in your area.

    Gym workout for you gym-rats or try a class at your gym.

Track your workout, time you spent and what you did.

_____

_____

Morning Meal (10mins) The most important meal of the day! No more muffins, doughnuts, or sugar filled cereals or eating nothing. Focus on healthy choices, like protein, fruit, and simple carbohydrates if you need that. Here are some choices or find some of your own. Just making one change to your breakfast, by replacing one item in your meal with a healthy one is a good start!

    Protein shake: Find one with 20 grams of protein and watch the sugar. Load her up, add coconut or almond milk instead of milk, add fruit (i.e.: banana, blueberry) or maybe some greens (i.e.: spinach, kale). This could be your nutrition filled meal that gets you going!

    3-4 Egg Whites, with onion, spinach or just plain, some blueberries and piece of toast (I personally don't like gluten, but your choice. There some good gluten free breads -give them a try!

    Protein bar: Make sure it has 20 grams of protein and watch the fat and sugar. I personally like Quest, Cliff, or Kind bars. One piece of fruit or handful of blueberries.

    Oatmeal: Try adding almond or coconut milk instead of milk, or don't add sugar. Add blueberries instead, or better yet, find a gluten-free oatmeal with almond milk, honey, and some almonds

Yum! Track what you ate and how you feel.

_____

_____

Important Things to Do Today

This may be a list of the key appointments today, Dr. Appt, interview, note times, etc.

_____

_____

WEEK TWO
DAY TWO

Date _____

Quiet Time (10mins) Chose 1 activity or find your own.
Practice Breathing: Take 5 deep breaths, breathing in deeply, breathing out deeply. Listen to your breath and tune into your body and how amazing it is!
Listen to a Meditation Ap.
Read some inspiring quotes from your favorite book or find someone to follow on Instagram that focuses on inspirational topics. My own meditation activity today was, track any thoughts:

_____

_____

Goal Setting (10 mins) Personal or professional goals.
What do you need to achieve today, keep it simple. These are your personal or professional goals that you are confident you can do if you put your mind to it. Goals can look like this: In the next year, open a coffee shop, be promoted in the next 3 months to the next level in my firm or clean out that closet in the kids room by the end of the week Writing this down helps you to be more intentional and focused!

_____

_____

Gratitude List (10 mins) Stop focusing on what's not working and start to see what is amazing in your life. This can look like: My morning coffee, sunrises, my kids, or that wonderful friend.

_____

_____

Morning Workout (20mins) Chose 1 activity or find your own.

Take a walk, walk the dog, walk up and down my stairs.
Get a yoga app and find some space in your family room or most yoga studios offer your first class for free, check one out in your area.

Gym workout for you gym-rats or try a class at your gym.
Track your workout, time you spent and what you did.

_____

_____

Morning Meal (10mins) The most important meal of the day! No more muffins, doughnuts, or sugar filled cereals or eating nothing. Focus on healthy choices, like protein, fruit, and simple carbohydrates if you need that. Here are some choices or find some of your own. Just making one change to your breakfast, by replacing one item in your meal with a healthy one is a good start!

Protein shake: Find one with 20 grams of protein and watch the sugar. Load her up, add coconut or almond milk instead of milk, add fruit (i.e.: banana, blueberry) or maybe some greens (i.e.: spinach, kale). This could be your nutrition filled meal that gets you going!

3-4 Egg Whites, with onion, spinach or just plain, some blueberries and piece of toast (I personally don't like gluten, but your choice. There some good gluten free breads -give them a try!

Protein bar: Make sure it has 20 grams of protein and watch the fat and sugar. I personally like Quest, Cliff, or Kind bars. One piece of fruit or handful of blueberries.

Oatmeal: Try adding almond or coconut milk instead of milk, or don't add sugar. Add blueberries instead, or better yet, find a gluten-free oatmeal with almond milk, honey, and some almonds
Yum! Track what you ate and how you feel.

_____

_____

Important Things to Do Today
This may be a list of the key appointments today, Dr. Appt, interview, note times etc.

_____

_____

WEEK TWO
DAY THREE

Date _____

Quiet Time (10mins) Chose 1 activity or find your own.

    Practice Breathing: Take 5 deep breaths, breathing in deeply, breathing out deeply. Listen to your breath and tune into your body and how amazing it is!

    Listen to a Meditation Ap.

    Read some inspiring quotes from your favorite book or find someone to follow on Instagram that focuses on inspirational topics.

    My own meditation activity today was, track any thoughts:

_____

_____

Goal Setting (10 mins) Personal or professional goals.

    What do you need to achieve today, keep it simple. These are your personal or professional goals that you are confident you can do if you put your mind to it. Goals can look like this: In the next year, open a coffee shop, be promoted in the next 3 months to the next level in my firm or clean out that closet in the kids room by the end of the week Writing this down helps you to be more intentional and focused!

_____

_____

Gratitude List (10 mins) Stop focusing on what's not working and start to see what is amazing in your life. This can look like: My morning coffee, sunrises, my kids, or that wonderful friend.

_____

_____

Morning Workout (20mins) Chose 1 activity or find your own.

Take a walk, walk the dog, walk up and down my stairs.
Get a yoga app and find some space in your family room or most yoga studios offer your first class for free, check one out in your area.

Gym workout for you gym-rats or try a class at your gym.
Track your workout, time you spent and what you did.

_____

_____

Morning Meal (10mins) The most important meal of the day! No more muffins, doughnuts, or sugar filled cereals or eating nothing. Focus on healthy choices, like protein, fruit, and simple carbohydrates if you need that. Here are some choices or find some of your own. Just making one change to your breakfast, by replacing one item in your meal with a healthy one is a good start!

Protein shake: Find one with 20 grams of protein and watch the sugar. Load her up, add coconut or almond milk instead of milk, add fruit (i.e.: banana, blueberry) or maybe some greens (i.e.: spinach, kale). This could be your nutrition filled meal that gets you going!

3-4 Egg Whites, with onion, spinach or just plain, some blueberries and piece of toast (I personally don't like gluten, but your choice. There some good gluten free breads -give them a try!

Protein bar: Make sure it has 20 grams of protein and watch the fat and sugar. I personally like Quest, Cliff, or Kind bars. One piece of fruit or handful of blueberries.

Oatmeal: Try adding almond or coconut milk instead of milk, or don't add sugar. Add blueberries instead, or better yet, find a gluten-free oatmeal with almond milk, honey, and some almonds

Yum! Track what you ate and how you feel.

_____

_____

Important Things to Do Today
This may be a list of the key appointments today, Dr. Appt, interview, note times, etc.

_____

_____

WEEK TWO

DAY FOUR

Date _____

Quiet Time (10mins) Chose 1 activity or find your own.

Practice Breathing: Take 5 deep breaths, breathing in deeply, breathing out deeply. Listen to your breath and tune into your body and how amazing it is!

Listen to a Meditation Ap.

Read some inspiring quotes from your favorite book or find someone to follow on Instagram that focuses on inspirational topics.

My own meditation activity today was, track any thoughts:

_____

_____

Goal Setting (10 mins) Personal or professional goals.

What do you need to achieve today, keep it simple. These are your personal or professional goals that you are confident you can do if you put your mind to it. Goals can look like this: In the next year, open a coffee shop, be promoted in the next 3 months to the next level in my firm or clean out that closet in the kids room by the end of the week Writing this down helps you to be more intentional and focused!

_____

_____

Gratitude List (10 mins) Stop focusing on what's not working and start to see what is amazing in your life. This can look like: My morning coffee, sunrises, my kids, or that wonderful friend.

_____

_____

Morning Workout (20mins) Chose 1 activity or find your own.

Take a walk, walk the dog, walk up and down my stairs.
Get a yoga app and find some space in your family room or most yoga studios offer your first class for free, check one out in your area.

Gym workout for you gym-rats or try a class at your gym.
Track your workout, time you spent and what you did.

_____

_____

Morning Meal (10mins) The most important meal of the day! No more muffins, doughnuts, or sugar filled cereals or eating nothing. Focus on healthy choices, like protein, fruit, and simple carbohydrates if you need that. Here are some choices or find some of your own. Just making one change to your breakfast, by replacing one item in your meal with a healthy one is a good start!

Protein shake: Find one with 20 grams of protein and watch the sugar. Load her up, add coconut or almond milk instead of milk, add fruit (i.e.: banana, blueberry) or maybe some greens (i.e.: spinach, kale). This could be your nutrition filled meal that gets you going!

3-4 Egg Whites, with onion, spinach or just plain, some blueberries and piece of toast (I personally don't like gluten, but your choice. There some good gluten free breads -give them a try!

Protein bar: Make sure it has 20 grams of protein and watch the fat and sugar. I personally like Quest, Cliff, or Kind bars. One piece of fruit or handful of blueberries.

Oatmeal: Try adding almond or coconut milk instead of milk, or don't add sugar. Add blueberries instead, or better yet, find a gluten-free oatmeal with almond milk, honey, and some almonds

Yum! Track what you ate and how you feel.

_____

_____

Important Things I To Do Today
This may be a list of the key appointments today, Dr appt, interview, note times.

_____

_____

WEEK TWO
DAY FIVE

Date _____

Quiet Time (10mins) Chose 1 activity or find your own.

Practice Breathing: Take 5 deep breaths, breathing in deeply, breathing out deeply. Listen to your breath and tune into your body and how amazing it is!

Listen to a Meditation Ap.

Read some inspiring quotes from your favorite book or find someone to follow on Instagram that focuses on inspirational topics.

My own meditation activity today was, track any thoughts:

_____

_____

Goal Setting (10 mins) Personal or professional goals.

What do you need to achieve today, keep it simple. These are your personal or professional goals that you are confident you can do if you put your mind to it. Goals can look like this: In the next year, open a coffee shop, be promoted in the next 3 months to the next level in my firm or clean out that closet in the kids room by the end of the week   Writing this down helps you to be more intentional and focused!

_____

_____

Gratitude List (10 mins) Stop focusing on what's not working and start to see what is amazing in your life. This can look like: My morning coffee, sunrises, my kids, or that wonderful friend.

_____

_____

Morning Workout (20mins) Chose 1 activity or find your own.

Take a walk, walk the dog, walk up and down my stairs.
Get a yoga app and find some space in your family room or most yoga studios offer your first class for free, check one out in your area.

Gym workout for you gym-rats or try a class at your gym. Track your workout, time you spent and what you did.

_____

_____

Morning Meal (10mins) The most important meal of the day! No more muffins, doughnuts, or sugar filled cereals or eating nothing. Focus on healthy choices, like protein, fruit, and simple carbohydrates if you need that. Here are some choices or find some of your own. Just making one change to your breakfast, by replacing one item in your meal with a healthy one is a good start!

Protein shake: Find one with 20 grams of protein and watch the sugar. Load her up, add coconut or almond milk instead of milk, add fruit (i.e.: banana, blueberry) or maybe some greens (i.e.: spinach, kale). This could be your nutrition filled meal that gets you going!

3-4 Egg Whites, with onion, spinach or just plain, some blueberries and piece of toast (I personally don't like gluten, but your choice. There some good gluten free breads -give them a try!

Protein bar: Make sure it has 20 grams of protein and watch the fat and sugar. I personally like Quest, Cliff, or Kind bars. One piece of fruit or handful of blueberries.

Oatmeal: Try adding almond or coconut milk instead of milk, or don't add sugar. Add blueberries instead, or better yet, find a gluten-free oatmeal with almond milk, honey, and some almonds

Yum! Track what you ate and how you feel.

_____

_____

Important Things I To Do Today
This may be a list of the key appointments today, Dr. Appt, interview, note times, etc.

_____

_____

WEEK THREE
DAY ONE

Date _____

Quiet Time (10mins) Chose 1 activity or find your own.

Practice Breathing: Lets dive deeper this week on this activity, find a breathing meditation app and stay focused for 10 minutes! Breathing is a huge stress reliever, I find doing this when stress hits, is amazing.

Listen to a Meditation app: I love the Abide app, lots of categories and choices or find one of your own, society today is disconnected spiritually, take that back!

Read some inspiring quotes from your favorite book or find someone to follow on Instagram that focuses on inspirational topics.

My own meditation activity today was, track any thoughts:

_____

_____

Goal Setting (10 mins) Personal or professional goals.

What do you need to achieve today, keep it simple. These are your personal or professional goals that you are confident you can do if you put your mind to it. Writing this down helps you to be more intentional!

_____

_____

Gratitude List (10 mins) Studies show that when you take just a few minutes to jot down those things in your life you are thankful for, you can recognize all the good in your life. It's time to count your blessings!

_____

_____

Morning Workout (20mins) Try a more rigorous workout this week, step it up a notch from last week. Chose 1 activity or one of your own.

Take a walk, walk the dog, try to run part of the time.

Get a yoga app and find some space in your family room.

Gym workout for you gym-rats, add some heavier weights or run on treadmill longer. Track your workout, time you spent and what you did.

_____

_____

Morning Meal (10mins) The most important meal of the day!

Protein shake: Find one with 20 grams of protein and watch the sugar. Load her up, add coconut or almond milk instead of milk, add fruit (i.e.: banana, blueberry) or maybe some greens (i.e.: spinach, kale). This could be your nutrition filled meal that gets you going! Try adding more spinach this week to your shake or some chia seeds.

3-4 Egg Whites, with onion, spinach or just plain, some blueberries and piece of toast (I personally don't like gluten), but it's your choice. There are some good gluten free breads -give them a try!

Try eating leftovers from last night dinner. That leftover chicken is delicious the next day!

Oatmeal: Try adding almond or coconut milk instead of milk, or don't add sugar. Add blueberries instead, or better yet, find a gluten-free oatmeal with almond milk, honey, and some almonds

Yum! Track what you ate and how you feel.

_____

_____

Important Things to Do Today

This may be a list of the key appointments today, Dr. Appt, interview, note times etc.

_____

_____

WEEK THREE
DAY TWO

Date _____

Quiet Time (10mins) Chose 1 activity or find your own.

Practice Breathing: Lets dive deeper this week on this activity, find a breathing meditation app and stay focused for 10 minutes! Breathing is a huge stress reliever, I find doing this when stress hits, is amazing.

Listen to a Meditation app: I love the Abide app, lots of categories and choices or find one of your own, society today is disconnected spiritually, take that back!

Read some inspiring quotes from your favorite book or find someone to follow on Instagram that focuses on inspirational topics.

My own meditation activity today was, track any thoughts:

_____

_____

Goal Setting (10 mins) Personal or professional goals.

What do you need to achieve today, keep it simple. These are your personal or professional goals that you are confident you can do if you put your mind to it. Writing this down helps you to be more intentional!

_____

_____

Gratitude List (10 mins) Studies show that when you take just a few minutes to jot down those things in your life you are thankful for, you can recognize all the good in your life. It's time to count your blessings!

_____

_____

Morning Workout (20mins) Try a more rigorous workout this week, step it up a notch from last week. Chose 1 activity or one of your own.

Take a walk, walk the dog, try to run part of the time.

Get a yoga app and find some space in your family room.

Gym workout for you gym-rats, add some heavier weights or run on treadmill longer. Track your workout, time you spent and what you did.

_____

_____

Morning Meal (10mins) The most important meal of the day!

Protein shake: Find one with 20 grams of protein and watch the sugar. Load her up, add coconut or almond milk instead of milk, add fruit (i.e.: banana, blueberry) or maybe some greens (i.e.: spinach, kale). This could be your nutrition filled meal that gets you going! Try adding more spinach this week to your shake or some chia seeds.

3-4 Egg Whites, with onion, spinach or just plain, some blueberries and piece of toast (I personally don't like gluten), but it's your choice. There are some good gluten free breads -give them a try!

Try eating leftovers from last night dinner. That leftover chicken is delicious the next day!

Oatmeal: Try adding almond or coconut milk instead of milk, or don't add sugar. Add blueberries instead, or better yet, find a gluten-free oatmeal with almond milk, honey, and some almonds
Yum! Track what you ate and how you feel.

_____

_____

Important Things to Do Today
This may be a list of the key appointments today, Dr. Appt, interview, note times, etc.

_____

_____

WEEK THREE
DAY THREE

Date _____

Quiet Time (10mins) Chose 1 activity or find your own.

Practice Breathing: Lets dive deeper this week on this activity, find a breathing meditation app and stay focused for 10 minutes! Breathing is a huge stress reliever, I find doing this when stress hits, is amazing.

Listen to a Meditation app: I love the Abide app, lots of categories and choices or find one of your own, society today is disconnected spiritually, take that back!

Read some inspiring quotes from your favorite book or find someone to follow on Instagram that focuses on inspirational topics.

My own meditation activity today was, track any thoughts:

_____

_____

Goal Setting (10 mins) Personal or professional goals.

What do you need to achieve today, keep it simple. These are your personal or professional goals that you are confident you can do if you put your mind to it. Writing this down helps you to be more intentional!

_____

_____

Gratitude List (10 mins) Studies show that when you take just a few minutes to jot down those things in your life you are thankful for, you can recognize all the good in your life. It's time to count your blessings!

_____

_____

Morning Workout (20mins) Try a more rigorous workout this week, step it up a notch from last week. Chose 1 activity or one of your own.

Take a walk, walk the dog, try to run part of the time.

Get a yoga app and find some space in your family room.

Gym workout for you gym-rats, add some heavier weights or run on treadmill longer. Track your workout, time you spent and what you did.

_____

_____

Morning Meal (10mins) The most important meal of the day!

Protein shake: Find one with 20 grams of protein and watch the sugar. Load her up, add coconut or almond milk instead of milk, add fruit (i.e.: banana, blueberry) or maybe some greens (i.e.: spinach, kale). This could be your nutrition filled meal that gets you going! Try adding more spinach this week to your shake or some chia seeds.

3-4 Egg Whites, with onion, spinach or just plain, some blueberries and piece of toast (I personally don't like gluten), but it's your choice. There are some good gluten free breads -give them a try!

Try eating leftovers from last night dinner. That leftover chicken is delicious the next day!

Oatmeal: Try adding almond or coconut milk instead of milk, or don't add sugar. Add blueberries instead, or better yet, find a gluten-free oatmeal with almond milk, honey, and some almonds

Yum! Track what you ate and how you feel.

_____

_____

Important Things to Do Today

This may be a list of the key appointments today, Dr. Appt, interview, note times, etc.

_____

_____

WEEK THREE
DAY FOUR

Date _____

Quiet Time (10mins) Chose 1 activity or find your own.

Practice Breathing: Lets dive deeper this week on this activity, find a breathing meditation app and stay focused for 10 minutes! Breathing is a huge stress reliever, I find doing this when stress hits, is amazing.

Listen to a Meditation app: I love the Abide app, lots of categories and choices or find one of your own, society today is disconnected spiritually, take that back!

Read some inspiring quotes from your favorite book or find someone to follow on Instagram that focuses on inspirational topics.

My own meditation activity today was, track any thoughts:

_____

_____

Goal Setting (10 mins) Personal or professional goals.

What do you need to achieve today, keep it simple. These are your personal or professional goals that you are confident you can do if you put your mind to it. Writing this down helps you to be more intentional!

_____

_____

Gratitude List (10 mins) Studies show that when you take just a few minutes to jot down those things in your life you are thankful for, you can recognize all the good in your life. It's time to count your blessings!

_____

_____

Morning Workout (20mins) Try a more rigorous workout this week, step it up a notch from last week. Chose 1 activity or one of your own.

Take a walk, walk the dog, try to run part of the time.

Get a yoga app and find some space in your family room.

Gym workout for you gym-rats, add some heavier weights or run on treadmill longer. Track your workout, time you spent and what you did.

_____

_____

Morning Meal (10mins) The most important meal of the day!

Protein shake: Find one with 20 grams of protein and watch the sugar. Load her up, add coconut or almond milk instead of milk, add fruit (i.e.: banana, blueberry) or maybe some greens (i.e.: spinach, kale). This could be your nutrition filled meal that gets you going! Try adding more spinach this week to your shake or some chia seeds.

3-4 Egg Whites, with onion, spinach or just plain, some blueberries and piece of toast (I personally don't like gluten), but it's your choice. There are some good gluten free breads -give them a try!

Try eating leftovers from last night dinner. That leftover chicken is delicious the next day!

Oatmeal: Try adding almond or coconut milk instead of milk, or don't add sugar. Add blueberries instead, or better yet, find a gluten-free oatmeal with almond milk, honey, and some almonds

Yum! Track what you ate and how you feel.

_____

_____

Important Things to Do Today

This may be a list of the key appointments today, Dr. Appt, interview, note times, etc.

_____

_____

WEEK THREE
DAY FIVE

Date _____

Quiet Time (10mins) Chose 1 activity or find your own.

Practice Breathing: Lets dive deeper this week on this activity, find a breathing meditation app and stay focused for 10 minutes! Breathing is a huge stress reliever, I find doing this when stress hits, is amazing.

Listen to a Meditation app: I love the Abide app, lots of categories and choices or find one of your own, society today is disconnected spiritually, take that back!

Read some inspiring quotes from your favorite book or find someone to follow on Instagram that focuses on inspirational topics.

My own meditation activity today was, track any thoughts:

_____

_____

Goal Setting (10 mins) Personal or professional goals.

What do you need to achieve today, keep it simple. These are your personal or professional goals that you are confident you can do if you put your mind to it. Writing this down helps you to be more intentional!

_____

_____

Gratitude List (10 mins) Studies show that when you take just a few minutes to jot down those things in your life you are thankful for, you can recognize all the good in your life. It's time to count your blessings!

_____

_____

Morning Workout (20mins) Try a more rigorous workout this week, step it up a notch from last week. Chose 1 activity or one of your own.

Take a walk, walk the dog, try to run part of the time.

Get a yoga app and find some space in your family room.

Gym workout for you gym-rats, add some heavier weights or run on treadmill longer. Track your workout, time you spent and what you did.

_____

_____

Morning Meal (10mins) The most important meal of the day!

Protein shake: Find one with 20 grams of protein and watch the sugar. Load her up, add coconut or almond milk instead of milk, add fruit (i.e.: banana, blueberry) or maybe some greens (i.e.: spinach, kale). This could be your nutrition filled meal that gets you going! Try adding more spinach this week to your shake or some chia seeds.

3-4 Egg Whites, with onion, spinach or just plain, some blueberries and piece of toast (I personally don't like gluten), but it's your choice. There are some good gluten free breads -give them a try!

Try eating leftovers from last night dinner. That leftover chicken is delicious the next day!

Oatmeal: Try adding almond or coconut milk instead of milk, or don't add sugar. Add blueberries instead, or better yet, find a gluten-free oatmeal with almond milk, honey, and some almonds

Yum! Track what you ate and how you feel.

_____

_____

Important Things to Do Today

This may be a list of the key appointments today, Dr. Appt, interview, note times, etc.

_____

_____

WEEK FOUR
DAY ONE

Date _____

Quiet Time (10mins) Chose 1 activity or find your own.

    Practice Breathing: Lets dive deeper this week on this activity, find a breathing meditation app and stay focused for 10 minutes! Breathing is a huge stress reliever, I find doing this when stress hits, is amazing.

    Listen to a Meditation app: I love the Abide app, lots of categories and choices or find one of your own, society today is disconnected spiritually, take that back!

    Read some inspiring quotes from your favorite book or find someone to follow on Instagram that focuses on inspirational topics.

    My own meditation activity today was, track any thoughts:

_____

_____

Goal Setting (10 mins) Personal or professional goals.

    Let's go deeper this week with goals, what are your goals for the week? Or maybe for the next 3 months or 6 months? What do you want to achieve, what have you been dreaming of doing, but just thought you really couldn't do it? This can be anything from getting a new job, to taking that vacation you have always dreamed of. Be realistic. But stopping talking about it and start doing something to achieve what you really want in life. Writing it down daily is powerful!

_____

_____

Gratitude List (10 mins) Studies show that when you take just a few minutes to jot down those things in your life you are thankful for, you can recognize all the good in your life. It's time to count your blessings!

_____

_____

Morning Workout (20mins) Try a more rigorous workout this week, step it up a notch from last week. Chose 1 activity or one of your own.

Take a walk, walk the dog, try to run part of the time.

Get a yoga app and find some space in your family room.

Gym workout for you gym-rats, add some heavier weights or run on treadmill longer. Track your workout, time you spent and what you did.

_____

_____

Morning Meal (10mins) The most important meal of the day!

Protein shake: Find one with 20 grams of protein and watch the sugar. Load her up, add coconut or almond milk instead of milk, add fruit (i.e.: banana, blueberry) or maybe some greens (i.e.: spinach, kale). This could be your nutrition filled meal that gets you going! Try adding more spinach this week to your shake or some chia seeds.

3-4 Egg Whites, with onion, spinach or just plain, some blueberries and piece of toast (I personally don't like gluten), but it's your choice. There are some good gluten free breads -give them a try!

Try eating leftovers from last night dinner. That leftover chicken is delicious the next day!

Oatmeal: Try adding almond or coconut milk instead of milk, or don't add sugar. Add blueberries instead, or better yet, find a gluten-free oatmeal with almond milk, honey, and some almonds

Yum! Track what you ate and how you feel.

_____

_____

Important Things to Do Today

This may be a list of the key appointments today, Dr. Appt, interview, note times, etc.

_____

_____

WEEK FOUR
DAY TWO

Date _____

Quiet Time (10mins) Chose 1 activity or find your own.

    Practice Breathing: Lets dive deeper this week on this activity, find a breathing meditation app and stay focused for 10 minutes! Breathing is a huge stress reliever, I find doing this when stress hits, is amazing.

    Listen to a Meditation app: I love the Abide app, lots of categories and choices or find one of your own, society today is disconnected spiritually, take that back!

    Read some inspiring quotes from your favorite book or find someone to follow on Instagram that focuses on inspirational topics.

    My own meditation activity today was, track any thoughts:

_____

_____

Goal Setting (10 mins) Personal or professional goals.

    Let's go deeper this week with goals, what are your goals for the week? Or maybe for the next 3 months or 6 months? What do you want to achieve, what have you been dreaming of doing, but just thought you really couldn't do it? This can be anything from getting a new job, to taking that vacation you have always dreamed of. Be realistic. But stopping talking about it and start doing something to achieve what you really want in life. Writing it down daily is powerful!

_____

_____

Gratitude List (10 mins) Studies show that when you take just a few minutes to jot down those things in your life you are thankful for, you can recognize all the good in your life. It's time to count your blessings!

_____

_____

Morning Workout (20mins) Try a more rigorous workout this week, step it up a notch from last week. Chose 1 activity or one of your own.

Take a walk, walk the dog, try to run part of the time.

Get a yoga app and find some space in your family room.

Gym workout for you gym-rats, add some heavier weights or run on treadmill longer. Track your workout, time you spent and what you did.

_____

_____

Morning Meal (10mins) The most important meal of the day!

Protein shake: Find one with 20 grams of protein and watch the sugar. Load her up, add coconut or almond milk instead of milk, add fruit (i.e.: banana, blueberry) or maybe some greens (i.e.: spinach, kale). This could be your nutrition filled meal that gets you going! Try adding more spinach this week to your shake or some chia seeds.

3-4 Egg Whites, with onion, spinach or just plain, some blueberries and piece of toast (I personally don't like gluten), but it's your choice. There are some good gluten free breads -give them a try!

Try eating leftovers from last night dinner. That leftover chicken is delicious the next day!

Oatmeal: Try adding almond or coconut milk instead of milk, or don't add sugar. Add blueberries instead, or better yet, find a gluten-free oatmeal with almond milk, honey, and some almonds

Yum! Track what you ate and how you feel.

_____

_____

Important Things to Do Today

This may be a list of the key appointments today, Dr. Appt, interview, note times, etc.

_____

_____

WEEK FOUR
DAY THREE

Date _____

Quiet Time (10mins) Chose 1 activity or find your own.

Practice Breathing: Lets dive deeper this week on this activity, find a breathing meditation app and stay focused for 10 minutes! Breathing is a huge stress reliever, I find doing this when stress hits, is amazing.

Listen to a Meditation app: I love the Abide app, lots of categories and choices or find one of your own, society today is disconnected spiritually, take that back!

Read some inspiring quotes from your favorite book or find someone to follow on Instagram that focuses on inspirational topics.

My own meditation activity today was, track any thoughts:

_____

_____

Goal Setting (10 mins) Personal or professional goals.

Let's go deeper this week with goals, what are your goals for the week? Or maybe for the next 3 months or 6 months? What do you want to achieve, what have you been dreaming of doing, but just thought you really couldn't do it? This can be anything from getting a new job, to taking that vacation you have always dreamed of. Be realistic. But stopping talking about it and start doing something to achieve what you really want in life. Writing it down daily is powerful!

_____

_____

Gratitude List (10 mins) Studies show that when you take just a few minutes to jot down those things in your life you are thankful for, you can recognize all the good in your life. It's time to count your blessings!

_____

_____

Morning Workout (20mins) Try a more rigorous workout this week, step it up a notch from last week. Chose 1 activity or one of your own.

Take a walk, walk the dog, try to run part of the time.

Get a yoga app and find some space in your family room.

Gym workout for you gym-rats, add some heavier weights or run on treadmill longer. Track your workout, time you spent and what you did.

_____

_____

Morning Meal (10mins) The most important meal of the day!

Protein shake: Find one with 20 grams of protein and watch the sugar. Load her up, add coconut or almond milk instead of milk, add fruit (i.e.: banana, blueberry) or maybe some greens (i.e.: spinach, kale). This could be your nutrition filled meal that gets you going! Try adding more spinach this week to your shake or some chia seeds.

3-4 Egg Whites, with onion, spinach or just plain, some blueberries and piece of toast (I personally don't like gluten), but it's your choice. There are some good gluten free breads -give them a try!

Try eating leftovers from last night dinner. That leftover chicken is delicious the next day!

Oatmeal: Try adding almond or coconut milk instead of milk, or don't add sugar. Add blueberries instead, or better yet, find a gluten-free oatmeal with almond milk, honey, and some almonds

Yum! Track what you ate and how you feel.

_____

_____

Important Things to Do Today

This may be a list of the key appointments today, Dr. Appt, interview, note times, etc.

_____

_____

WEEK FOUR
DAY FOUR

Date _____

Quiet Time (10mins) Chose 1 activity or find your own.

Practice Breathing: Lets dive deeper this week on this activity, find a breathing meditation app and stay focused for 10 minutes! Breathing is a huge stress reliever, I find doing this when stress hits, is amazing.

Listen to a Meditation app: I love the Abide app, lots of categories and choices or find one of your own, society today is disconnected spiritually, take that back!

Read some inspiring quotes from your favorite book or find someone to follow on Instagram that focuses on inspirational topics.

My own meditation activity today was, track any thoughts:

_____

_____

Goal Setting (10 mins) Personal or professional goals.

Let's go deeper this week with goals, what are your goals for the week? Or maybe for the next 3 months or 6 months? What do you want to achieve, what have you been dreaming of doing, but just thought you really couldn't do it? This can be anything from getting a new job, to taking that vacation you have always dreamed of. Be realistic. But stopping talking about it and start doing something to achieve what you really want in life. Writing it down daily is powerful!

_____

_____

Gratitude List (10 mins) Studies show that when you take just a few minutes to jot down those things in your life you are thankful for, you can recognize all the good in your life. It's time to count your blessings!

_____

_____

Morning Workout (20mins) Try a more rigorous workout this week, step it up a notch from last week. Chose 1 activity or one of your own.

Take a walk, walk the dog, try to run part of the time.

Get a yoga app and find some space in your family room.

Gym workout for you gym-rats, add some heavier weights or run on treadmill longer. Track your workout, time you spent and what you did.

_____

_____

Morning Meal (10mins) The most important meal of the day!

Protein shake: Find one with 20 grams of protein and watch the sugar. Load her up, add coconut or almond milk instead of milk, add fruit (i.e.: banana, blueberry) or maybe some greens (i.e.: spinach, kale). This could be your nutrition filled meal that gets you going! Try adding more spinach this week to your shake or some chia seeds.

3-4 Egg Whites, with onion, spinach or just plain, some blueberries and piece of toast (I personally don't like gluten), but it's your choice. There are some good gluten free breads -give them a try!

Try eating leftovers from last night dinner. That leftover chicken is delicious the next day!

Oatmeal: Try adding almond or coconut milk instead of milk, or don't add sugar. Add blueberries instead, or better yet, find a gluten-free oatmeal with almond milk, honey, and some almonds

Yum! Track what you ate and how you feel.

_____

_____

Important Things to Do Today
This may be a list of the key appointments today, Dr. Appt, interview, note times, etc.

_____

_____

WEEK FOUR
DAY FIVE

Date _____

Quiet Time (10mins) Chose 1 activity or find your own.

Practice Breathing: Lets dive deeper this week on this activity, find a breathing meditation app and stay focused for 10 minutes! Breathing is a huge stress reliever, I find doing this when stress hits, is amazing.

Listen to a Meditation app: I love the Abide app, lots of categories and choices or find one of your own, society today is disconnected spiritually, take that back!

Read some inspiring quotes from your favorite book or find someone to follow on Instagram that focuses on inspirational topics.

My own meditation activity today was, track any thoughts:

_____

_____

Goal Setting (10 mins) Personal or professional goals.

Let's go deeper this week with goals, what are your goals for the week? Or maybe for the next 3 months or 6 months? What do you want to achieve, what have you been dreaming of doing, but just thought you really couldn't do it? This can be anything from getting a new job, to taking that vacation you have always dreamed of. Be realistic. But stopping talking about it and start doing something to achieve what you really want in life. Writing it down daily is powerful!

_____

_____

Gratitude List (10 mins) Studies show that when you take just a few minutes to jot down those things in your life you are thankful for, you can recognize all the good in your life. It's time to count your blessings!

_____

_____

Morning Workout (20mins) Try a more rigorous workout this week, step it up a notch from last week. Chose 1 activity or one of your own.

Take a walk, walk the dog, try to run part of the time.

Get a yoga app and find some space in your family room.

Gym workout for you gym-rats, add some heavier weights or run on treadmill longer. Track your workout, time you spent and what you did.

_____

_____

Morning Meal (10mins) The most important meal of the day!

Protein shake: Find one with 20 grams of protein and watch the sugar. Load her up, add coconut or almond milk instead of milk, add fruit (i.e.: banana, blueberry) or maybe some greens (i.e.: spinach, kale). This could be your nutrition filled meal that gets you going! Try adding more spinach this week to your shake or some chia seeds.

3-4 Egg Whites, with onion, spinach or just plain, some blueberries and piece of toast (I personally don't like gluten), but it's your choice. There are some good gluten free breads -give them a try!

Try eating leftovers from last night dinner. That leftover chicken is delicious the next day!

Oatmeal: Try adding almond or coconut milk instead of milk, or don't add sugar. Add blueberries instead, or better yet, find a gluten-free oatmeal with almond milk, honey, and some almonds

Yum! Track what you ate and how you feel.

_____

_____

Important Things to Do Today

This may be a list of the key appointments today, Dr. Appt, interview, note times, etc.

_____

_____

WEEK FIVE
DAY ONE

Date _____

Quiet Time (10mins) Chose 1 activity or find your own.

Practice Breathing: Repeat last week's activity. Listen to your breath and tune into your body and how amazing it is!

Listen to a Meditation app: I love the Abide app, lots of categories and choices or find one that you may like.

Connecting with our spiritual emotions is powerful, try praying and focusing on how you feel or what you hear, prayer changed my life, write down your prayers.

My own meditation activity today was, track any thoughts:

_____

_____

Goal Setting (10 mins) Personal or professional goals.

Let's go deeper this week with goals, what are your goals for the week? Or maybe for the next 3 months or 6 months? What do you want to achieve, what have you been dreaming of doing, but just thought you really couldn't do it? This can be anything from getting a new job, to taking that vacation you have always dreamed of. Be realistic. But stopping talking about it and start doing something to achieve what you really want in life. Writing it down daily is powerful!

_____

_____

Gratitude List (10 mins). I hope you aren't skipping this activity, focusing on the good in your life can change your attitude- being positive is uplifting and simply nice to be around.

_____

_____

Morning Workout (20mins) Try a more rigorous workout this week, step it up a notch from last week. Chose 1 activity that is harder than last week activity or chose your own but push yourself harder this week.

Walk, walk the dog, try to run part of the time, run more this week.

Get a yoga app and find some space in your family room.

Gym workout for you gym-rats, add some heavier weights or run on treadmill longer. Track your workout, time you spent and what you did.

_____

_____

Morning Meal (10mins) I tend to eat the same thing, try something different this week, chose a different meal or one of your own, keep it healthy!

Protein shake: Find one with 20 grams of protein and watch the sugar. Try some different add-ins, a different milk or coconut water, add a different fruit this week or maybe a different green. Don't be afraid to switch it up!

3-4 Egg Whites, with onion, spinach or just plain, some blueberries and piece of toast (I personally don't like gluten), but it's your choice. There are some good gluten free breads -give them a try!

Try eating leftovers from last night dinner that leftover chicken is delicious the next day!

Oatmeal: Try adding almond or coconut milk instead of milk, or don't add sugar. Add blueberries instead, or better yet, find a gluten-free oatmeal with almond milk, honey, and some almonds
Yum! Track what you ate and how you feel.

_____

_____

Important Things to Do Today

_____

_____

WEEK FIVE
DAY TWO

Date _____

Quiet Time (10mins) Chose 1 activity or find your own.

Practice Breathing: Repeat last week's activity. Listen to your breath and tune into your body and how amazing it is!

Listen to a Meditation app: I love the Abide app, lots of categories and choices or find one that you may like.

Connecting with our spiritual emotions is powerful, try praying and focusing on how you feel or what you hear, prayer changed my life, write down your prayers.

_____

_____

Goal Setting (10 mins) Personal or professional goals.

Let's go deeper this week with goals, what are your goals for the week? Or maybe for the next 3 months or 6 months? What do you want to achieve, what have you been dreaming of doing, but just thought you really couldn't do it? This can be anything from getting a new job, to taking that vacation you have always dreamed of. Be realistic. But stopping talking about it and start doing something to achieve what you really want in life. Writing it down daily is powerful!

_____

_____

Gratitude List (10 mins). I hope you aren't skipping this activity, focusing on the good in your life can change your attitude- being positive is uplifting and simply nice to be around.

_____

_____

Morning Workout (20mins) Try a more rigorous workout this week, step it up a notch from last week. Chose 1 activity that is harder than last week activity or chose your own but push yourself harder this week.

Walk, walk the dog, try to run part of the time, run more this week.

Get a yoga app and find some space in your family room.

Gym workout for you gym-rats, add some heavier weights or run on treadmill longer. Track your workout, time you spent and what you did.

Morning Meal (10mins) I tend to eat the same thing, try something different this week, chose a different meal or one of your own, keep it healthy!

Protein shake: Find one with 20 grams of protein and watch the sugar. Try some different add-ins, a different milk or coconut water, add a different fruit this week or maybe a different green. Don't be afraid to switch it up!

3-4 Egg Whites, with onion, spinach or just plain, some blueberries and piece of toast (I personally don't like gluten), but it's your choice. There are some good gluten free breads -give them a try!

Try eating leftovers from last night dinner that leftover chicken is delicious the next day!

Oatmeal: Try adding almond or coconut milk instead of milk, or don't add sugar. Add blueberries instead, or better yet, find a gluten-free oatmeal with almond milk, honey, and some almonds
Yum! Track what you ate and how you feel.

Important Things to Do Today

96

WEEK FIVE
DAY THREE

Date _____

Quiet Time (10mins) Chose 1 activity or find your own.
    Practice Breathing: Repeat last week's activity. Listen to your breath and tune into your body and how amazing it is!
    Listen to a Meditation app: I love the Abide app, lots of categories and choices or find one that you may like.
    Connecting with our spiritual emotions is powerful, try praying and focusing on how you feel or what you hear, prayer changed my life, write down your prayers.

_____

_____

Goal Setting (10 mins) Personal or professional goals.
    Let's go deeper this week with goals, what are your goals for the week? Or maybe for the next 3 months or 6 months? What do you want to achieve, what have you been dreaming of doing, but just thought you really couldn't do it? This can be anything from getting a new job, to taking that vacation you have always dreamed of. Be realistic. But stopping talking about it and start doing something to achieve what you really want in life. Writing it down daily is powerful!

_____

_____

Gratitude List (10 mins). I hope you aren't skipping this activity, focusing on the good in your life can change your attitude- being positive is uplifting and simply nice to be around.

_____

_____

Morning Workout (20mins) Try a more rigorous workout this week, step it up a notch from last week. Chose 1 activity that is harder than last week activity or chose your own but push yourself harder this week.

Walk, walk the dog, try to run part of the time, run more this week.

Get a yoga app and find some space in your family room.

Gym workout for you gym-rats, add some heavier weights or run on treadmill longer. Track your workout, time you spent and what you did.

_____

_____

Morning Meal (10mins) I tend to eat the same thing, try something different this week, chose a different meal or one of your own, keep it healthy!

Protein shake: Find one with 20 grams of protein and watch the sugar. Try some different add-ins, a different milk or coconut water, add a different fruit this week or maybe a different green. Don't be afraid to switch it up!

3-4 Egg Whites, with onion, spinach or just plain, some blueberries and piece of toast (I personally don't like gluten), but it's your choice. There are some good gluten free breads -give them a try!

Try eating leftovers from last night dinner that leftover chicken is delicious the next day!

Oatmeal: Try adding almond or coconut milk instead of milk, or don't add sugar. Add blueberries instead, or better yet, find a gluten-free oatmeal with almond milk, honey, and some almonds
Yum! Track what you ate and how you feel.

_____

_____

Important Things to Do Today

_____

_____

WEEK FIVE
DAY FOUR

Date _____

Quiet Time (10mins) Chose 1 activity or find your own.
　　Practice Breathing: Repeat last week's activity. Listen to your breath and tune into your body and how amazing it is!
　　Listen to a Meditation app: I love the Abide app, lots of categories and choices or find one that you may like.
　　Connecting with our spiritual emotions is powerful, try praying and focusing on how you feel or what you hear, prayer changed my life, write down your prayers.

_____

_____

Goal Setting (10 mins) Personal or professional goals.
　　Let's go deeper this week with goals, what are your goals for the week? Or maybe for the next 3 months or 6 months? What do you want to achieve, what have you been dreaming of doing, but just thought you really couldn't do it? This can be anything from getting a new job, to taking that vacation you have always dreamed of. Be realistic. But stopping talking about it and start doing something to achieve what you really want in life. Writing it down daily is powerful!

_____

_____

Gratitude List (10 mins). I hope you aren't skipping this activity, focusing on the good in your life can change your attitude- being positive is uplifting and simply nice to be around.

_____

_____

Morning Workout (20mins) Try a more rigorous workout this week, step it up a notch from last week. Chose 1 activity that is harder than last week activity or chose your own but push yourself harder this week.

Walk, walk the dog, try to run part of the time, run more this week.

Get a yoga app and find some space in your family room.

Gym workout for you gym-rats, add some heavier weights or run on treadmill longer. Track your workout, time you spent and what you did.

_____

_____

Morning Meal (10mins) I tend to eat the same thing, try something different this week, chose a different meal or one of your own, keep it healthy!

Protein shake: Find one with 20 grams of protein and watch the sugar. Try some different add-ins, a different milk or coconut water, add a different fruit this week or maybe a different green. Don't be afraid to switch it up!

3-4 Egg Whites, with onion, spinach or just plain, some blueberries and piece of toast (I personally don't like gluten), but it's your choice. There are some good gluten free breads -give them a try!

Try eating leftovers from last night dinner that leftover chicken is delicious the next day!

Oatmeal: Try adding almond or coconut milk instead of milk, or don't add sugar. Add blueberries instead, or better yet, find a gluten-free oatmeal with almond milk, honey, and some almonds
Yum! Track what you ate and how you feel.

_____

_____

Important Things to Do Today

_____

_____

WEEK FIVE
DAY FIVE

Date _____

Quiet Time (10mins) Chose 1 activity or find your own.

Practice Breathing: Repeat last week's activity. Listen to your breath and tune into your body and how amazing it is!

Listen to a Meditation app: I love the Abide app, lots of categories and choices or find one that you may like.

Connecting with our spiritual emotions is powerful, try praying and focusing on how you feel or what you hear, prayer changed my life, write down your prayers.

_____

_____

Goal Setting (10 mins) Personal or professional goals.

Let's go deeper this week with goals, what are your goals for the week? Or maybe for the next 3 months or 6 months? What do you want to achieve, what have you been dreaming of doing, but just thought you really couldn't do it? This can be anything from getting a new job, to taking that vacation you have always dreamed of. Be realistic. But stopping talking about it and start doing something to achieve what you really want in life. Writing it down daily is powerful!

_____

_____

Gratitude List (10 mins). I hope you aren't skipping this activity, focusing on the good in your life can change your attitude- being positive is uplifting and simply nice to be around.

_____

_____

Morning Workout (20mins) Try a more rigorous workout this week, step it up a notch from last week. Chose 1 activity that is harder than last week activity or chose your own but push yourself harder this week.

Walk, walk the dog, try to run part of the time, run more this week. Get a yoga app and find some space in your family room.

Gym workout for you gym-rats, add some heavier weights or run on treadmill longer. Track your workout, time you spent and what you did. Track what you did.

_____

_____

Morning Meal (10mins) I tend to eat the same thing, try something different this week, chose a different meal or one of your own, keep it healthy!

Protein shake: Find one with 20 grams of protein and watch the sugar. Try some different add-ins, a different milk or coconut water, add a different fruit this week or maybe a different green. Don't be afraid to switch it up!

3-4 Egg Whites, with onion, spinach or just plain, some blueberries and piece of toast (I personally don't like gluten), but it's your choice. There are some good gluten free breads -give them a try!

Try eating leftovers from last night dinner that leftover chicken is delicious the next day!

Oatmeal: Try adding almond or coconut milk instead of milk, or don't add sugar. Add blueberries instead, or better yet, find a gluten-free oatmeal with almond milk, honey, and some almonds
Yum! Track what you ate and how you feel.

_____

_____

Important Things to Do Today

_____

_____

WEEK SIX
DAY ONE

Date _____

Quiet Time (10mins) Chose 1 activity or find your own.

Practice Breathing: Repeat last week's activity. Listen to your breath and tune into your body and how amazing it is!

Listen to a Meditation app: I love the Abide app, lots of categories and choices or find one that you may like.

Connecting with our spiritual emotions is powerful, try praying and focusing how you feel or what you hear, prayer changed my life, write down your prayers.

_____

_____

Goal Setting (10 mins) Personal or professional goals.

Keep writing these goals down, don't give up on them! Progress takes time, energy and intention. Sometimes it's not the end result that really matters but what you are discovering about yourself on the journey.

_____

_____

Gratitude List (10 mins). It's time to count your blessings!

_____

_____

Morning Workout (20mins) Try a more rigorous workout this week, step it up a notch from last week. Chose 1 activity that is harder than last week activity or chose your own but push yourself harder this week.

Walk and add some sprint walks this week or try to run part of the time, if you have been running, run more this week.

Do yoga in your family room, go to a local yoga class (many studios offer free first-time sessions) or try Pilates, reformer Pilates is so fun and a body changer!

Gym workout-see my website for some great workout samples from a certified personal trainer, some can be done at home or a gym. Track what you did.

_____

_____

Morning Meal (10mins) I tend to eat the same thing, try something different this week, chose a different meal or one of your own, keep it healthy!

Protein shake: Find one with 20 grams of protein and watch the sugar. Try some different add-ins, a different milk or coconut water, add a different fruit this week or maybe a different green. Don't be afraid to switch it up!

3-4 Egg Whites, with onion, spinach or just plain, some blueberries and piece of toast (I personally don't like gluten, but your choice. There some good gluten free breads -give them a try!

Try eating leftovers from last night dinner that leftover chicken is delicious the next day!

Oatmeal: Try adding almond or coconut milk instead of milk, or don't add sugar. Add blueberries instead, or better yet, find a gluten-free oatmeal with almond milk, honey, and some almonds
Yum! Track what you ate and how you feel.

_____

_____

Important Things to Do Today

_____

_____

WEEK SIX
DAY TWO

Date _____

Quiet Time (10mins) Chose 1 activity or find your own.

Practice Breathing: Repeat last week's activity. Listen to your breath and tune into your body and how amazing it is!

Listen to a Meditation app: I love the Abide app, lots of categories and choices or find one that you may like.

Connecting with our spiritual emotions is powerful, try praying and focusing how you feel or what you hear, prayer changed my life, write down your prayers.

_____

_____

Goal Setting (10 mins) Personal or professional goals.

Keep writing these goals down, don't give up on them! Progress takes time, energy and intention. Sometimes it's not the end result that really matters but what you are discovering about yourself on the journey.

_____

_____

Gratitude List (10 mins). It's time to count your blessings!

_____

_____

Morning Workout (20mins) Try a more rigorous workout this week, step it up a notch from last week. Chose 1 activity that is harder than last week activity or chose your own but push yourself harder this week.

Walk and add some sprint walks this week or try to run part of the time, if you have been running, run more this week.

Do yoga in your family room, go to a local yoga class (many studios offer free first-time sessions) or try Pilates, reformer Pilates is so fun and a body changer!

Gym workout-see my website for some great workout samples from a certified personal trainer, some can be done at home or a gym. Track what you did.

_____

_____

Morning Meal (10mins) I tend to eat the same thing, try something different this week, chose a different meal or one of your own, keep it healthy!

Protein shake: Find one with 20 grams of protein and watch the sugar. Try some different add-ins, a different milk or coconut water, add a different fruit this week or maybe a different green. Don't be afraid to switch it up!

3-4 Egg Whites, with onion, spinach or just plain, some blueberries and piece of toast (I personally don't like gluten, but your choice. There some good gluten free breads -give them a try!

Try eating leftovers from last night dinner that leftover chicken is delicious the next day!

Oatmeal: Try adding almond or coconut milk instead of milk, or don't add sugar. Add blueberries instead, or better yet, find a gluten-free oatmeal with almond milk, honey, and some almonds
Yum! Track what you ate and how you feel.

_____

_____

Important Things to Do Today

_____

_____

WEEK SIX
DAY THREE

Date _____

Quiet Time (10mins) Chose 1 activity or find your own.
Practice Breathing: Repeat last week's activity. Listen to your breath and tune into your body and how amazing it is!
Listen to a Meditation app: I love the Abide app, lots of categories and choices or find one that you may like.
Connecting with our spiritual emotions is powerful, try praying and focusing how you feel or what you hear, prayer changed my life, write down your prayers.

_____

_____

Goal Setting (10 mins) Personal or professional goals.
Keep writing these goals down, don't give up on them! Progress takes time, energy and intention. Sometimes it's not the end result that really matters but what you are discovering about yourself on the journey.

_____

_____

Gratitude List (10 mins). It's time to count your blessings!

_____

_____

Morning Workout (20mins) Try a more rigorous workout this week, step it up a notch from last week. Chose 1 activity that is harder than last week activity or chose your own but push yourself harder this week.

Walk and add some sprint walks this week or try to run part of the time, if you have been running, run more this week.

Do yoga in your family room, go to a local yoga class (many studios offer free first-time sessions) or try Pilates, reformer Pilates is so fun and a body changer!

Gym workout-see my website for some great workout samples from a certified personal trainer, some can be done at home or a gym. Track what you did.

Morning Meal (10mins) I tend to eat the same thing, try something different this week, chose a different meal or one of your own, keep it healthy!

Protein shake: Find one with 20 grams of protein and watch the sugar. Try some different add-ins, a different milk or coconut water, add a different fruit this week or maybe a different green. Don't be afraid to switch it up!

3-4 Egg Whites, with onion, spinach or just plain, some blueberries and piece of toast (I personally don't like gluten, but your choice. There some good gluten free breads -give them a try!

Try eating leftovers from last night dinner that leftover chicken is delicious the next day!

Oatmeal: Try adding almond or coconut milk instead of milk, or don't add sugar. Add blueberries instead, or better yet, find a gluten-free oatmeal with almond milk, honey, and some almonds
Yum! Track what you ate and how you feel.

Important Things to Do Today

WEEK SIX
DAY FOUR

Date _____

Quiet Time (10mins) Chose 1 activity or find your own.

Practice Breathing: Repeat last week's activity. Listen to your breath and tune into your body and how amazing it is!

Listen to a Meditation app: I love the Abide app, lots of categories and choices or find one that you may like.

Connecting with our spiritual emotions is powerful, try praying and focusing how you feel or what you hear, prayer changed my life, write down your prayers.

_____

_____

Goal Setting (10 mins) Personal or professional goals.

Keep writing these goals down, don't give up on them! Progress takes time, energy and intention. Sometimes it's not the end result that really matters but what you are discovering about yourself on the journey.

_____

_____

Gratitude List (10 mins). It's time to count your blessings!

_____

_____

Morning Workout (20mins) Try a more rigorous workout this week, step it up a notch from last week. Chose 1 activity that is harder than last week activity or chose your own but push yourself harder this week.

Walk and add some sprint walks this week or try to run part of the time, if you have been running, run more this week.

Do yoga in your family room, go to a local yoga class (many studios offer free first-time sessions) or try Pilates, reformer Pilates is so fun and a body changer!

Gym workout-see my website for some great workout samples from a certified personal trainer, some can be done at home or a gym. Track what you did.

_____

_____

Morning Meal (10mins) I tend to eat the same thing, try something different this week, chose a different meal or one of your own, keep it healthy!

Protein shake: Find one with 20 grams of protein and watch the sugar. Try some different add-ins, a different milk or coconut water, add a different fruit this week or maybe a different green. Don't be afraid to switch it up!

3-4 Egg Whites, with onion, spinach or just plain, some blueberries and piece of toast (I personally don't like gluten, but your choice. There some good gluten free breads -give them a try!

Try eating leftovers from last night dinner that leftover chicken is delicious the next day!

Oatmeal: Try adding almond or coconut milk instead of milk, or don't add sugar. Add blueberries instead, or better yet, find a gluten-free oatmeal with almond milk, honey, and some almonds
Yum! Track what you ate and how you feel.

_____

_____

Important Things to Do Today

_____

_____

WEEK SIX
DAY FIVE

Date _____

Quiet Time (10mins) Chose 1 activity or find your own.

Practice Breathing: Repeat last week's activity. Listen to your breath and tune into your body and how amazing it is!

Listen to a Meditation app: I love the Abide app, lots of categories and choices or find one that you may like.

Connecting with our spiritual emotions is powerful, try praying and focusing how you feel or what you hear, prayer changed my life, write down your prayers.

_____

_____

Goal Setting (10 mins) Personal or professional goals.

Keep writing these goals down, don't give up on them! Progress takes time, energy and intention. Sometimes it's not the end result that really matters but what you are discovering about yourself on the journey.

_____

_____

Gratitude List (10 mins). It's time to count your blessings!

_____

_____

Morning Workout (20mins) Try a more rigorous workout this week, step it up a notch from last week. Chose 1 activity that is harder than last week activity or chose your own but push yourself harder this week.

Walk and add some sprint walks this week or try to run part of the time, if you have been running, run more this week.

Do yoga in your family room, go to a local yoga class (many studios offer free first-time sessions) or try Pilates, reformer Pilates is so fun and a body changer!

Gym workout-see my website for some great workout samples from a certified personal trainer, some can be done at home or a gym. Track what you did.

_____

_____

Morning Meal (10mins) I tend to eat the same thing, try something different this week, chose a different meal or one of your own, keep it healthy!

Protein shake: Find one with 20 grams of protein and watch the sugar. Try some different add-ins, a different milk or coconut water, add a different fruit this week or maybe a different green. Don't be afraid to switch it up!

3-4 Egg Whites, with onion, spinach or just plain, some blueberries and piece of toast (I personally don't like gluten, but your choice. There some good gluten free breads -give them a try!

Try eating leftovers from last night dinner that leftover chicken is delicious the next day!

Oatmeal: Try adding almond or coconut milk instead of milk, or don't add sugar. Add blueberries instead, or better yet, find a gluten-free oatmeal with almond milk, honey, and some almonds
Yum! Track what you ate and how you feel.

_____

_____

Important Things to Do Today

_____

_____

WEEK SEVEN
DAY ONE

Date _____

Quiet Time (10mins) Chose 1 activity or find your own.

Practice Breathing: Repeat last week's activity. Listen to your breath and tune into your body and how amazing it is!

Listen to a Meditation app: I love the Abide app, lots of categories and choices or find one that you may like.

Connecting with our spiritual emotions is powerful, try praying and focusing how you feel or what you hear, prayer changed my life, write down your prayers.

_____

_____

Goal Setting (10 mins) Personal or professional goals.

Be mindful of the steps it takes to achieve your goals, take one goal you have set from the last few weeks and now write down the specific steps you need to take to achieve these goals. For example, if your goal is to find a new job, write down in your notes update my resume, apply for some jobs today/this week or check out my website and schedule a career coaching session and discover where you may be falling short in the employment process; maybe you need to be improving your interviewing skills or being creative on how you apply for a job, do your homework here. Be specific.

_____

_____

Gratitude List (10 mins). It's time to count your blessings!

_____

_____

Morning Workout (20mins) Try a more rigorous workout this week, step it up a notch from last week. Chose 1 activity that is harder than last week activity or chose your own but push yourself harder this week.

Walk, walk faster this week (your doggie will love it!) or try to run part of the time or run even longer than last week.

Try a harder yoga or Pilates app and do 10 sits ups at the end.

Gym workout for you gym-rats, add some heavier weights or run on treadmill longer. Track your workout, time you spent and what you did.

_____

_____

Morning Meal (10mins) Remember, it's all about a healthy choice, but now maybe lunch can be healthy too! Try a chicken breast, green salad and some sweet potato, but watch portions! Or you can even do the recipes below for lunch, maybe do a shake for breakfast and the eggs for lunch or vice versa. Have fun with eating but be mindful, also focus on this week, eating real food, nothing packaged or processed.

Protein shake: Find one with 20 grams of protein and watch the sugar. Try some different add-ins, a different milk or coconut water, add a different fruit this week or maybe a different green. Don't be afraid to switch it up!

3-4 Egg Whites, with onion, spinach or just plain, some blueberries and piece of toast or a small sweet potato (even better!).

Try eating leftovers from last night dinner. That leftover chicken is delicious the next day!

Oatmeal: Try making your own oatmeal in crockpot, there are some great recipes out there for gluten free and they are delicious, you can make a batch and freeze some so you can have this for the entire week! Track what you eat and how you feel.

_____

_____

Important Things to Do Today

_____

_____

WEEK SEVEN
DAY TWO

Date _____

Quiet Time (10mins) Chose 1 activity or find your own.

Practice Breathing: Repeat last week's activity. Listen to your breath and tune into your body and how amazing it is!

Listen to a Meditation app: I love the Abide app, lots of categories and choices or find one that you may like.

Connecting with our spiritual emotions is powerful, try praying and focusing how you feel or what you hear, prayer changed my life, write down your prayers.

_____

_____

Goal Setting (10 mins) Personal or professional goals.

Be mindful of the steps it takes to achieve your goals, take one goal you have set from the last few weeks and now write down the specific steps you need to take to achieve these goals. For example, if your goal is to find a new job, write down in your notes update my resume, apply for some jobs today/this week or check out my website and schedule a career coaching session and discover where you may be falling short in the employment process; maybe you need to be improving your interviewing skills or being creative on how you apply for a job, do your homework here. Be specific.

_____

_____

Gratitude List (10 mins). It's time to count your blessings!

_____

_____

Morning Workout (20mins) Try a more rigorous workout this week, step it up a notch from last week. Chose 1 activity that is harder than last week activity or chose your own but push yourself harder this week.

Walk, walk faster this week (your doggie will love it!) or try to run part of the time or run even longer than last week.

Try a harder yoga or Pilates app and do 10 sits ups at the end.

Gym workout for you gym-rats, add some heavier weights or run on treadmill longer. Track your workout, time you spent and what you did.

_____

_____

Morning Meal (10mins) Remember, it's all about a healthy choice, but now maybe lunch can be healthy too! Try a chicken breast, green salad and some sweet potato, but watch portions! Or you can even do the recipes below for lunch, maybe do a shake for breakfast and the eggs for lunch or vice versa. Have fun with eating but be mindful, also focus on this week, eating real food, nothing packaged or processed.

Protein shake: Find one with 20 grams of protein and watch the sugar. Try some different add-ins, a different milk or coconut water, add a different fruit this week or maybe a different green. Don't be afraid to switch it up!

3-4 Egg Whites, with onion, spinach or just plain, some blueberries and piece of toast or a small sweet potato (even better!).

Try eating leftovers from last night dinner. That leftover chicken is delicious the next day!

Oatmeal: Try making your own oatmeal in crockpot, there are some great recipes out there for gluten free and they are delicious, you can make a batch and freeze some so you can have this for the entire week! Track what you eat and how you feel.

_____

_____

Important Things to Do Today

_____

_____

WEEK SEVEN
DAY THREE

Date _____

Quiet Time (10mins) Chose 1 activity or find your own.

Practice Breathing: Repeat last week's activity. Listen to your breath and tune into your body and how amazing it is!

Listen to a Meditation app: I love the Abide app, lots of categories and choices or find one that you may like.

Connecting with our spiritual emotions is powerful, try praying and focusing how you feel or what you hear, prayer changed my life, write down your prayers.

_____

_____

Goal Setting (10 mins) Personal or professional goals.

Be mindful of the steps it takes to achieve your goals, take one goal you have set from the last few weeks and now write down the specific steps you need to take to achieve these goals. For example, if your goal is to find a new job, write down in your notes update my resume, apply for some jobs today/this week or check out my website and schedule a career coaching session and discover where you may be falling short in the employment process; maybe you need to be improving your interviewing skills or being creative on how you apply for a job, do your homework here. Be specific.

_____

_____

Gratitude List (10 mins). It's time to count your blessings!

_____

_____

Morning Workout (20mins) Try a more rigorous workout this week, step it up a notch from last week. Chose 1 activity that is harder than last week activity or chose your own but push yourself harder this week.

Walk, walk faster this week (your doggie will love it!) or try to run part of the time or run even longer than last week.

Try a harder yoga or Pilates app and do 10 sits ups at the end.

Gym workout for you gym-rats, add some heavier weights or run on treadmill longer. Track your workout, time you spent and what you did.

Morning Meal (10mins) Remember, it's all about a healthy choice, but now maybe lunch can be healthy too! Try a chicken breast, green salad and some sweet potato, but watch portions! Or you can even do the recipes below for lunch, maybe do a shake for breakfast and the eggs for lunch or vice versa. Have fun with eating but be mindful, also focus on this week, eating real food, nothing packaged or processed.

Protein shake: Find one with 20 grams of protein and watch the sugar. Try some different add-ins, a different milk or coconut water, add a different fruit this week or maybe a different green. Don't be afraid to switch it up!

3-4 Egg Whites, with onion, spinach or just plain, some blueberries and piece of toast or a small sweet potato (even better!).

Try eating leftovers from last night dinner. That leftover chicken is delicious the next day!

Oatmeal: Try making your own oatmeal in crockpot, there are some great recipes out there for gluten free and they are delicious, you can make a batch and freeze some so you can have this for the entire week! Track what you eat and how you feel.

Important Things to Do Today

WEEK SEVEN
DAY FOUR

Date _____

Quiet Time (10mins) Chose 1 activity or find your own.

Practice Breathing: Repeat last week's activity. Listen to your breath and tune into your body and how amazing it is!

Listen to a Meditation app: I love the Abide app, lots of categories and choices or find one that you may like.

Connecting with our spiritual emotions is powerful, try praying and focusing how you feel or what you hear, prayer changed my life, write down your prayers.

_____

_____

Goal Setting (10 mins) Personal or professional goals.

Be mindful of the steps it takes to achieve your goals, take one goal you have set from the last few weeks and now write down the specific steps you need to take to achieve these goals. For example, if your goal is to find a new job, write down in your notes update my resume, apply for some jobs today/this week or check out my website and schedule a career coaching session and discover where you may be falling short in the employment process; maybe you need to be improving your interviewing skills or being creative on how you apply for a job, do your homework here. Be specific.

_____

_____

Gratitude List (10 mins). It's time to count your blessings!

_____

_____

Morning Workout (20mins) Try a more rigorous workout this week, step it up a notch from last week. Chose 1 activity that is harder than last week activity or chose your own but push yourself harder this week.

Walk, walk faster this week (your doggie will love it!) or try to run part of the time or run even longer than last week.

Try a harder yoga or Pilates app and do 10 sits ups at the end.

Gym workout for you gym-rats, add some heavier weights or run on treadmill longer. Track your workout, time you spent and what you did.

_____

_____

Morning Meal (10mins) Remember, it's all about a healthy choice, but now maybe lunch can be healthy too! Try a chicken breast, green salad and some sweet potato, but watch portions! Or you can even do the recipes below for lunch, maybe do a shake for breakfast and the eggs for lunch or vice versa. Have fun with eating but be mindful, also focus on this week, eating real food, nothing packaged or processed.

Protein shake: Find one with 20 grams of protein and watch the sugar. Try some different add-ins, a different milk or coconut water, add a different fruit this week or maybe a different green. Don't be afraid to switch it up!

3-4 Egg Whites, with onion, spinach or just plain, some blueberries and piece of toast or a small sweet potato (even better!).

Try eating leftovers from last night dinner. That leftover chicken is delicious the next day!

Oatmeal: Try making your own oatmeal in crockpot, there are some great recipes out there for gluten free and they are delicious, you can make a batch and freeze some so you can have this for the entire week! Track what you eat and how you feel.

_____

_____

Important Things to Do Today

_____

_____

WEEK SEVEN
DAY FIVE

Date _____

Quiet Time (10mins) Chose 1 activity or find your own.

Practice Breathing: Repeat last week's activity. Listen to your breath and tune into your body and how amazing it is!

Listen to a Meditation app: I love the Abide app, lots of categories and choices or find one that you may like.

Connecting with our spiritual emotions is powerful, try praying and focusing how you feel or what you hear, prayer changed my life, write down your prayers.

_____

_____

Goal Setting (10 mins) Personal or professional goals.

Be mindful of the steps it takes to achieve your goals, take one goal you have set from the last few weeks and now write down the specific steps you need to take to achieve these goals. For example, if your goal is to find a new job, write down in your notes update my resume, apply for some jobs today/this week or check out my website and schedule a career coaching session and discover where you may be falling short in the employment process; maybe you need to be improving your interviewing skills or being creative on how you apply for a job, do your homework here. Be specific.

_____

_____

Gratitude List (10 mins). It's time to count your blessings!

_____

_____

Morning Workout (20mins) Try a more rigorous workout this week, step it up a notch from last week. Chose 1 activity that is harder than last week activity or chose your own but push yourself harder this week.

Walk, walk faster this week (your doggie will love it!) or try to run part of the time or run even longer than last week.

Try a harder yoga or Pilates app and do 10 sits ups at the end.

Gym workout for you gym-rats, add some heavier weights or run on treadmill longer. Track your workout, time you spent and what you did.

_____

_____

Morning Meal (10mins) Remember, it's all about a healthy choice, but now maybe lunch can be healthy too! Try a chicken breast, green salad and some sweet potato, but watch portions! Or you can even do the recipes below for lunch, maybe do a shake for breakfast and the eggs for lunch or vice versa. Have fun with eating but be mindful, also focus on this week, eating real food, nothing packaged or processed.

Protein shake: Find one with 20 grams of protein and watch the sugar. Try some different add-ins, a different milk or coconut water, add a different fruit this week or maybe a different green. Don't be afraid to switch it up!

3-4 Egg Whites, with onion, spinach or just plain, some blueberries and piece of toast or a small sweet potato (even better!).

Try eating leftovers from last night dinner. That leftover chicken is delicious the next day!

Oatmeal: Try making your own oatmeal in crockpot, there are some great recipes out there for gluten free and they are delicious, you can make a batch and freeze some so you can have this for the entire week! Track what you eat and how you feel.

_____

_____

Important Things to Do Today

_____

_____

WEEK EIGHT
DAY ONE

Date _____

Quiet Time (10mins) Chose 1 activity or find your own.

Practice Breathing: Repeat last week's activity. Listen to your breath and tune into your body and how amazing it is!

Listen to a Meditation app: I love the Abide app, lots of categories and choices or find one that you may like.

Connecting with our spiritual emotions is powerful, try praying and focusing how you feel or what you hear, prayer changed my life, write down your prayers.

_____

_____

Goal Setting (10 mins) Personal or professional goals.

Be mindful of the steps it takes to achieve your goals, take one goal you have set from the last few weeks and now write down the specific steps you need to take to achieve these goals. For example, if your goal is to find a new job, write down in your notes update my resume, apply for some jobs today/this week or check out my website and schedule a career coaching session and discover where you may be falling short in the employment process; maybe you need to be improving your interviewing skills or being creative on how you apply for a job, do your homework here. Be specific.

_____

_____

Gratitude List (10 mins). It's time to count your blessings!

_____

_____

Morning Workout (20mins) Try a more rigorous workout this week, step it up a notch from last week. Chose 1 activity that is harder than last week activity or chose your own but push yourself harder this week.

Walk, walk faster this week (your doggie will love it!) or try to run part of the time or run even longer than last week.

Try a harder yoga or Pilates app and do 10 sits ups at the end.

Gym workout for you gym-rats, add some heavier weights or run on treadmill longer. Track your workout, time you spent and what you did.

_____

_____

Morning Meal (10mins) Remember, it's all about a healthy choice, but now maybe lunch can be healthy too! Try a chicken breast, green salad and some sweet potato, but watch portions! Or you can even do the recipes below for lunch, maybe do a shake for breakfast and the eggs for lunch or vice versa. Have fun with eating but be mindful, also focus on this week, eating real food, nothing packaged or processed.

Protein shake: Find one with 20 grams of protein and watch the sugar. Try some different add-ins, a different milk or coconut water, add a different fruit this week or maybe a different green. Don't be afraid to switch it up!

3-4 Egg Whites, with onion, spinach or just plain, some blueberries and piece of toast or a small sweet potato (even better!).

Try eating leftovers from last night dinner. That leftover chicken is delicious the next day!

Oatmeal: Try making your own oatmeal in crockpot, there are some great recipes out there for gluten free and they are delicious, you can make a batch and freeze some so you can have this for the entire week! Track what you eat and how you feel.

_____

_____

Important Things to Do Today

_____

_____

WEEK EIGHT
DAY TWO

Date _____

Quiet Time (10mins) Chose 1 activity or find your own.

Practice Breathing: Do this breathing activity and combine it with another, maybe one below or one of your choice, but allow 10 minutes.

Listen to a Meditation app: Abide app or chose from meditation app of choice.

Connecting with our spiritual emotions is powerful. Try praying and focusing how you feel or what you hear. Write down your prayers and see if they get answered.

My own meditation activity today was, track any thoughts:

_____

_____

Goal Setting (10 mins) Personal or professional goals.

Be mindful of the steps it takes to achieve your goals, take one goal you have set from the last few weeks and now write down the specific steps you need to take to achieve these goals. For example, if your goal is to find a new job, write down in your notes update my resume, apply for some jobs today/this week or check out my website and schedule a career coaching session and discover where you may be falling short in the employment process; maybe you need to be improving your interviewing skills or being creative on how you apply for a job, do your homework here. Be specific.

_____

_____

Gratitude List (10 mins). It's time to count your blessings!

_____

_____

Morning Workout (20mins) Try a more rigorous workout this week, step it up a notch from last week. Chose 1 activity that is harder than last week activity or chose your own but push yourself harder this week.

Walk, walk faster this week (your doggie will love it!) or try to run part of the time or run even longer than last week.

Try a harder yoga or Pilates app and do 10 sits ups at the end.

Gym workout for you gym-rats, add some heavier weights or run on treadmill longer. Track your workout, time you spent and what you did.

_____

_____

Morning Meal (10mins) Remember, it's all about a healthy choice, but now maybe lunch can be healthy too! Try a chicken breast, green salad and some sweet potato, but watch portions! Or you can even do the recipes below for lunch, maybe do a shake for breakfast and the eggs for lunch or vice versa. Have fun with eating but be mindful, also focus on this week, eating real food, nothing packaged or processed.

Protein shake: Find one with 20 grams of protein and watch the sugar. Try some different add-ins, a different milk or coconut water, add a different fruit this week or maybe a different green. Don't be afraid to switch it up!

3-4 Egg Whites, with onion, spinach or just plain, some blueberries and piece of toast or a small sweet potato (even better!).

Try eating leftovers from last night dinner. That leftover chicken is delicious the next day!

Oatmeal: Try making your own oatmeal in crockpot, there are some great recipes out there for gluten free and they are delicious, you can make a batch and freeze some so you can have this for the entire week! Track what you eat and how you feel.

_____

_____

Important Things to Do Today

_____

_____

WEEK EIGHT
DAY THREE

Date _____

Quiet Time (10mins) Chose 1 activity or find your own.

Practice Breathing: Do this breathing activity and combine it with another, maybe one below or one of your choice, but allow 10 minutes.

Listen to a Meditation app: Abide app or chose from meditation app of choice.

Connecting with our spiritual emotions is powerful. Try praying and focusing how you feel or what you hear. Write down your prayers and see if they get answered.

My own meditation activity today was, track any thoughts:

_____

_____

Goal Setting (10 mins) Personal or professional goals.

Be mindful of the steps it takes to achieve your goals, take one goal you have set from the last few weeks and now write down the specific steps you need to take to achieve these goals. For example, if your goal is to find a new job, write down in your notes update my resume, apply for some jobs today/this week or check out my website and schedule a career coaching session and discover where you may be falling short in the employment process; maybe you need to be improving your interviewing skills or being creative on how you apply for a job, do your homework here. Be specific.

_____

_____

Gratitude List (10 mins). It's time to count your blessings!

_____

_____

Morning Workout (20mins) Try a more rigorous workout this week, step it up a notch from last week. Chose 1 activity that is harder than last week activity or chose your own but push yourself harder this week.

Walk, walk faster this week (your doggie will love it!) or try to run part of the time or run even longer than last week.

Try a harder yoga or Pilates app and do 10 sits ups at the end.

Gym workout for you gym-rats, add some heavier weights or run on treadmill longer. Track your workout, time you spent and what you did.

_____

_____

Morning Meal (10mins) Remember, it's all about a healthy choice, but now maybe lunch can be healthy too! Try a chicken breast, green salad and some sweet potato, but watch portions! Or you can even do the recipes below for lunch, maybe do a shake for breakfast and the eggs for lunch or vice versa. Have fun with eating but be mindful, also focus on this week, eating real food, nothing packaged or processed.

Protein shake: Find one with 20 grams of protein and watch the sugar. Try some different add-ins, a different milk or coconut water, add a different fruit this week or maybe a different green. Don't be afraid to switch it up!

3-4 Egg Whites, with onion, spinach or just plain, some blueberries and piece of toast or a small sweet potato (even better!).

Try eating leftovers from last night dinner. That leftover chicken is delicious the next day!

Oatmeal: Try making your own oatmeal in crockpot, there are some great recipes out there for gluten free and they are delicious, you can make a batch and freeze some so you can have this for the entire week! Track what you eat and how you feel.

_____

_____

Important Things to Do Today

_____

_____

WEEK EIGHT
DAY FOUR

Date _____

Quiet Time (10mins) Chose 1 activity or find your own.

Practice Breathing: Do this breathing activity and combine it with another, maybe one below or one of your choice, but allow 10 minutes.

Listen to a Meditation app: Abide app or chose from meditation app of choice.

Connecting with our spiritual emotions is powerful. Try praying and focusing how you feel or what you hear. Write down your prayers and see if they get answered.

My own meditation activity today was, track any thoughts:

_____

_____

Goal Setting (10 mins) Personal or professional goals.

Be mindful of the steps it takes to achieve your goals, take one goal you have set from the last few weeks and now write down the specific steps you need to take to achieve these goals. For example, if your goal is to find a new job, write down in your notes update my resume, apply for some jobs today/this week or check out my website and schedule a career coaching session and discover where you may be falling short in the employment process; maybe you need to be improving your interviewing skills or being creative on how you apply for a job, do your homework here. Be specific.

_____

_____

Gratitude List (10 mins). It's time to count your blessings!

_____

_____

Morning Workout (20mins) Try a more rigorous workout this week, step it up a notch from last week. Chose 1 activity that is harder than last week activity or chose your own but push yourself harder this week.

Walk, walk faster this week (your doggie will love it!) or try to run part of the time or run even longer than last week.

Try a harder yoga or Pilates app and do 10 sits ups at the end.

Gym workout for you gym-rats, add some heavier weights or run on treadmill longer. Track your workout, time you spent and what you did.

_____

_____

Morning Meal (10mins) Remember, it's all about a healthy choice, but now maybe lunch can be healthy too! Try a chicken breast, green salad and some sweet potato, but watch portions! Or you can even do the recipes below for lunch, maybe do a shake for breakfast and the eggs for lunch or vice versa. Have fun with eating but be mindful, also focus on this week, eating real food, nothing packaged or processed.

Protein shake: Find one with 20 grams of protein and watch the sugar. Try some different add-ins, a different milk or coconut water, add a different fruit this week or maybe a different green. Don't be afraid to switch it up!

3-4 Egg Whites, with onion, spinach or just plain, some blueberries and piece of toast or a small sweet potato (even better!).

Try eating leftovers from last night dinner. That leftover chicken is delicious the next day!

Oatmeal: Try making your own oatmeal in crockpot, there are some great recipes out there for gluten free and they are delicious, you can make a batch and freeze some so you can have this for the entire week! Track what you eat and how you feel.

_____

_____

Important Things to Do Today

_____

_____

WEEK EIGHT
DAY FIVE

Date _____

Quiet Time (10mins) Chose 1 activity or find your own.

    Practice Breathing: Do this breathing activity and combine it with another, maybe one below or one of your choice, but allow 10 minutes.

    Listen to a Meditation app: Abide app or chose from meditation app of choice.

    Connecting with our spiritual emotions is powerful. Try praying and focusing how you feel or what you hear. Write down your prayers and see if they get answered.

    My own meditation activity today was, track any thoughts:

_____

_____

Goal Setting (10 mins) Personal or professional goals.

    Be mindful of the steps it takes to achieve your goals, take one goal you have set from the last few weeks and now write down the specific steps you need to take to achieve these goals. For example, if your goal is to find a new job, write down in your notes update my resume, apply for some jobs today/this week or check out my website and schedule a career coaching session and discover where you may be falling short in the employment process; maybe you need to be improving your interviewing skills or being creative on how you apply for a job, do your homework here. Be specific.

_____

_____

Gratitude List (10 mins). It's time to count your blessings!

_____

_____

Morning Workout (20mins) Try a more rigorous workout this week, step it up a notch from last week. Chose 1 activity that is harder than last week activity or chose your own but push yourself harder this week.

Walk, walk faster this week (your doggie will love it!) or try to run part of the time or run even longer than last week.

Try a harder yoga or Pilates app and do 10 sits ups at the end.

Gym workout for you gym-rats, add some heavier weights or run on treadmill longer. Track your workout, time you spent and what you did.

Morning Meal (10mins) Remember, it's all about a healthy choice, but now maybe lunch can be healthy too! Try a chicken breast, green salad and some sweet potato, but watch portions! Or you can even do the recipes below for lunch, maybe do a shake for breakfast and the eggs for lunch or vice versa. Have fun with eating but be mindful, also focus on this week, eating real food, nothing packaged or processed.

Protein shake: Find one with 20 grams of protein and watch the sugar. Try some different add-ins, a different milk or coconut water, add a different fruit this week or maybe a different green. Don't be afraid to switch it up!

3-4 Egg Whites, with onion, spinach or just plain, some blueberries and piece of toast or a small sweet potato (even better!).

Try eating leftovers from last night dinner. That leftover chicken is delicious the next day!

Oatmeal: Try making your own oatmeal in crockpot, there are some great recipes out there for gluten free and they are delicious, you can make a batch and freeze some so you can have this for the entire week! Track what you eat and how you feel.

Important Things to Do Today

WEEK NINE
DAY ONE

Date _____

Quiet Time (10mins) Chose 1 activity or find your own.

Practice Breathing: Do breathing activity for 5 mins and try a meditation app for 5 mins, shake it up!

Listen to a Meditation app: Abide app or chose from meditation app of choice.

Connecting with our spiritual emotions is powerful, try praying and focusing how you feel or what you hear. Go back to earlier weeks, review your prayers, have some of them been answered? Pretty cool, huh?

My own meditation activity today was, track any thoughts:

_____

_____

Goal Setting (10 mins) Be mindful of the steps it takes to achieve your goals, take one goal you have set from the last few weeks and now write down the specific steps you need to take to achieve these goals. For example, if your goal is to find a new job, write down in your notes update my resume, apply for some jobs today/this week or check out my website and schedule a career coaching session and discover where you may be falling short in the employment process; maybe you need to be improving your interviewing skills or being creative on how you apply for a job, do your homework here. Be specific.

_____

_____

Gratitude List (10 mins). It's time to count your blessings!

_____

_____

Morning Workout (20mins) Try a more rigorous workout this week, step it up a notch from last week. Chose 1 activity that is harder than last week's activity or chose your own but push yourself harder this week.

Walk, walk faster this week (your doggie will love it!) or try to run part of the time or run even longer than last week.

Try a harder yoga or Pilates app and do 10 sits ups at the end or add a 3 min jog.

Gym workout, combo of weights and cardio. Try adding in a yoga class this week instead of gym, just one day, yoga is a great way to control stress, many studios offer free first classes, give it a try. Track your workout, time you spent and what you did.

_____

_____

Morning Meal (10mins) Remember, it's all about a healthy choice in the morning, but now maybe lunch can be healthy too! Try a chicken breast, green salad and some sweet potato, but watch portions! You can do these for lunch too, maybe shake for breakfast and the eggs for lunch or vice versa.

Protein shake: See my website for some great recipes.

3-4 Egg Whites, with onion, spinach or just plain, some blueberries and piece of toast or a small sweet potato. (even better!)

Try eating leftovers from last night dinner. That leftover chicken is delicious the next day!

Oatmeal or try another healthy cereal with a non-dairy milk. Dairy is not your friend, so try to move to coconut, almond milk or another non-dairy beverage of your choice. Track what you eat and how you feel.

_____

_____

Important Things to Do Today

_____

_____

WEEK NINE
DAY TWO

Date _____

Quiet Time (10mins) Chose 1 activity or find your own.

Practice Breathing: Do breathing activity for 5 mins and try a meditation app for 5 mins, shake it up!

Listen to a Meditation app: Abide app or chose from meditation app of choice.

Connecting with our spiritual emotions is powerful, try praying and focusing how you feel or what you hear. Go back to earlier weeks, review your prayers, have some of them been answered? Pretty cool, huh?

My own meditation activity today was, track any thoughts:

_____

_____

Goal Setting (10 mins) Be mindful of the steps it takes to achieve your goals, take one goal you have set from the last few weeks and now write down the specific steps you need to take to achieve these goals. For example, if your goal is to find a new job, write down in your notes update my resume, apply for some jobs today/this week or check out my website and schedule a career coaching session and discover where you may be falling short in the employment process; maybe you need to be improving your interviewing skills or being creative on how you apply for a job, do your homework here. Be specific.

_____

_____

Gratitude List (10 mins). It's time to count your blessings!

_____

_____

175

Morning Workout (20mins) Try a more rigorous workout this week, step it up a notch from last week. Chose 1 activity that is harder than last week's activity or chose your own but push yourself harder this week.

Walk, walk faster this week (your doggie will love it!) or try to run part of the time or run even longer than last week.

Try a harder yoga or Pilates app and do 10 sits ups at the end or add a 3 min jog.

Gym workout, combo of weights and cardio. Try adding in a yoga class this week instead of gym, just one day, yoga is a great way to control stress, many studios offer free first classes, give it a try. Track your workout, time you spent and what you did.

Morning Meal (10mins) Remember, it's all about a healthy choice in the morning, but now maybe lunch can be healthy too! Try a chicken breast, green salad and some sweet potato, but watch portions! You can do these for lunch too, maybe shake for breakfast and the eggs for lunch or vice versa.

Protein shake: See my website for some great recipes.

3-4 Egg Whites, with onion, spinach or just plain, some blueberries and piece of toast or a small sweet potato. (even better!)

Try eating leftovers from last night dinner. That leftover chicken is delicious the next day!

Oatmeal or try another healthy cereal with a non-dairy milk. Dairy is not your friend, so try to move to coconut, almond milk or another non-dairy beverage of your choice. Track what you eat and how you feel.

Important Things to Do Today

WEEK NINE
DAY THREE

Date _____

Quiet Time (10mins) Chose 1 activity or find your own.

Practice Breathing: Do breathing activity for 5 mins and try a meditation app for 5 mins, shake it up!

Listen to a Meditation app: Abide app or chose from meditation app of choice.

Connecting with our spiritual emotions is powerful, try praying and focusing how you feel or what you hear. Go back to earlier weeks, review your prayers, have some of them been answered? Pretty cool, huh?

My own meditation activity today was, track any thoughts:

_____

_____

Goal Setting (10 mins) Be mindful of the steps it takes to achieve your goals, take one goal you have set from the last few weeks and now write down the specific steps you need to take to achieve these goals. For example, if your goal is to find a new job, write down in your notes update my resume, apply for some jobs today/this week or check out my website and schedule a career coaching session and discover where you may be falling short in the employment process; maybe you need to be improving your interviewing skills or being creative on how you apply for a job, do your homework here. Be specific.

_____

_____

Gratitude List (10 mins). It's time to count your blessings!

_____

_____

Morning Workout (20mins) Try a more rigorous workout this week, step it up a notch from last week. Chose 1 activity that is harder than last week's activity or chose your own but push yourself harder this week.

Walk, walk faster this week (your doggie will love it!) or try to run part of the time or run even longer than last week.

Try a harder yoga or Pilates app and do 10 sits ups at the end or add a 3 min jog.

Gym workout, combo of weights and cardio. Try adding in a yoga class this week instead of gym, just one day, yoga is a great way to control stress, many studios offer free first classes, give it a try. Track your workout, time you spent and what you did.

_____

_____

Morning Meal (10mins) Remember, it's all about a healthy choice in the morning, but now maybe lunch can be healthy too! Try a chicken breast, green salad and some sweet potato, but watch portions! You can do these for lunch too, maybe shake for breakfast and the eggs for lunch or vice versa.

Protein shake: See my website for some great recipes.

3-4 Egg Whites, with onion, spinach or just plain, some blueberries and piece of toast or a small sweet potato. (even better!)

Try eating leftovers from last night dinner. That leftover chicken is delicious the next day!

Oatmeal or try another healthy cereal with a non-dairy milk. Dairy is not your friend, so try to move to coconut, almond milk or another non-dairy beverage of your choice. Track what you eat and how you feel.

_____

_____

Important Things to Do Today

_____

_____

WEEK NINE
DAY FOUR

Date _____

Quiet Time (10mins) Chose 1 activity or find your own.

Practice Breathing: Do breathing activity for 5 mins and try a meditation app for 5 mins, shake it up!

Listen to a Meditation app: Abide app or chose from meditation app of choice.

Connecting with our spiritual emotions is powerful, try praying and focusing how you feel or what you hear. Go back to earlier weeks, review your prayers, have some of them been answered? Pretty cool, huh?

My own meditation activity today was, track any thoughts:

_____

_____

Goal Setting (10 mins) Be mindful of the steps it takes to achieve your goals, take one goal you have set from the last few weeks and now write down the specific steps you need to take to achieve these goals. For example, if your goal is to find a new job, write down in your notes update my resume, apply for some jobs today/this week or check out my website and schedule a career coaching session and discover where you may be falling short in the employment process; maybe you need to be improving your interviewing skills or being creative on how you apply for a job, do your homework here. Be specific.

_____

_____

Gratitude List (10 mins). It's time to count your blessings!

_____

_____

183

Morning Workout (20mins) Try a more rigorous workout this week, step it up a notch from last week. Chose 1 activity that is harder than last week's activity or chose your own but push yourself harder this week.

Walk, walk faster this week (your doggie will love it!) or try to run part of the time or run even longer than last week.

Try a harder yoga or Pilates app and do 10 sits ups at the end or add a 3 min jog.

Gym workout, combo of weights and cardio. Try adding in a yoga class this week instead of gym, just one day, yoga is a great way to control stress, many studios offer free first classes, give it a try. Track your workout, time you spent and what you did.

_____

_____

Morning Meal (10mins) Remember, it's all about a healthy choice in the morning, but now maybe lunch can be healthy too! Try a chicken breast, green salad and some sweet potato, but watch portions! You can do these for lunch too, maybe shake for breakfast and the eggs for lunch or vice versa.

Protein shake: See my website for some great recipes.

3-4 Egg Whites, with onion, spinach or just plain, some blueberries and piece of toast or a small sweet potato. (even better!)

Try eating leftovers from last night dinner. That leftover chicken is delicious the next day!

Oatmeal or try another healthy cereal with a non-dairy milk. Dairy is not your friend, so try to move to coconut, almond milk or another non-dairy beverage of your choice. Track what you eat and how you feel.

_____

_____

Important Things to Do Today

_____

_____

WEEK NINE
DAY FIVE

Date _____

Quiet Time (10mins) Chose 1 activity or find your own.

Practice Breathing: Do breathing activity for 5 mins and try a meditation app for 5 mins, shake it up!

Listen to a Meditation app: Abide app or chose from meditation app of choice.

Connecting with our spiritual emotions is powerful, try praying and focusing how you feel or what you hear. Go back to earlier weeks, review your prayers, have some of them been answered? Pretty cool, huh?

My own meditation activity today was, track any thoughts:

_____

_____

Goal Setting (10 mins) Be mindful of the steps it takes to achieve your goals, take one goal you have set from the last few weeks and now write down the specific steps you need to take to achieve these goals. For example, if your goal is to find a new job, write down in your notes update my resume, apply for some jobs today/this week or check out my website and schedule a career coaching session and discover where you may be falling short in the employment process; maybe you need to be improving your interviewing skills or being creative on how you apply for a job, do your homework here. Be specific.

_____

_____

Gratitude List (10 mins). It's time to count your blessings!

_____

_____

Morning Workout (20mins) Try a more rigorous workout this week, step it up a notch from last week. Chose 1 activity that is harder than last week's activity or chose your own but push yourself harder this week.

Walk, walk faster this week (your doggie will love it!) or try to run part of the time or run even longer than last week.

Try a harder yoga or Pilates app and do 10 sits ups at the end or add a 3 min jog.

Gym workout, combo of weights and cardio. Try adding in a yoga class this week instead of gym, just one day, yoga is a great way to control stress, many studios offer free first classes, give it a try. Track your workout, time you spent and what you did.

_____

_____

Morning Meal (10mins) Remember, it's all about a healthy choice in the morning, but now maybe lunch can be healthy too! Try a chicken breast, green salad and some sweet potato, but watch portions! You can do these for lunch too, maybe shake for breakfast and the eggs for lunch or vice versa.

Protein shake: See my website for some great recipes.

3-4 Egg Whites, with onion, spinach or just plain, some blueberries and piece of toast or a small sweet potato. (even better!)

Try eating leftovers from last night dinner. That leftover chicken is delicious the next day!

Oatmeal or try another healthy cereal with a non-dairy milk. Dairy is not your friend, so try to move to coconut, almond milk or another non-dairy beverage of your choice. Track what you eat and how you feel.

_____

_____

Important Things to Do Today

_____

_____

WEEK TEN
DAY ONE

You are almost done. Congratulations for committing one hour per day for the last 10 weeks to self-care and finding your success! Success varies amongst individuals. For some it may be the job promotion or finding a new job, for others it may be losing weight, feeling more energy or just finding more peace and balance in their day. Take a minute to reflect on where you were on Week 1 and where you are today! I can imagine that if you truly committed to this journal with an open mind, you are experiencing success! **BUT DON'T STOP NOW, GO TO MY WEBSITE** journalwaytosuccess.com **AND ORDER YOUR NEXT 3 MONTH JOURNAL AND SUCCESS WILL CONTINUE TO FLOW!**

Date _____

Quiet Time (10mins) Chose 1 activity or find your own.

Practice Breathing: Do breathing activity for 5 mins and try a meditation app for 5 mins, shake it up!

Listen to a Meditation app: Abide app or app of choice.

Pray, journal your prayers.

My own meditation activity today was, track any thoughts:

_____

_____

Goal Setting (10 mins) Continue to focus on that goal you set last week. I once heard a "goal is a dream with a deadline".

Write down that goals each day this week. Continue to list the steps it takes to achieve that goal, remember baby steps are key, list those steps, note the ones you have completed. Be specific.

_____

_____

Gratitude List (10 mins). It's time to count your blessings!

_____

_____

Morning Workout (20mins) Keep up the hard work! If you are pushing yourself, stick to it this week, don't give up now!

    Walk or run, it doesn't matter, just move your body for 20 mins.

    Yoga or other class you enjoy.

    Gym-Did you push yourself in your workouts last week? Then keep it up this week, hard work can change your body, energy level and confidence so you can go kill that interview, land that new sales account or keep up with those busy kiddos. Repeat last week or chose a different sample workout created by a certified trainer on my website.

_____

_____

Morning Meal (10mins) If you have committed to removing processed food, even one or two items in your diet/at each meal and replaced them with real healthy food, I can imagine you are seeing a difference in not only your energy but maybe in those jeans too! Try not only eating a healthy breakfast and lunch but now try eating a healthy dinner too! It may take a little planning, but a little planning can go a long way and your family may thank you too! Check out my website for some good recipes for breakfast, lunch and dinner created by certified nutrition coach.

Track what you eat and how you feel.

_____

_____

Important Things to Do Today

_____

_____

WEEK TEN
DAY TWO

Date _____

Quiet Time (10mins) Chose 1 activity or find your own.

Practice Breathing: Do breathing activity for 5 mins and try a meditation app for 5 mins, shake it up!

Listen to a Meditation app: Abide app or app of choice.

Pray, journal your prayers.

My own meditation activity today was, track any thoughts:

_____

_____

Goal Setting (10 mins) Continue to focus on that goal you set last week. I once heard a "goal is a dream with a deadline."

Write down that goal each day this week. Continue to list the steps it takes to achieve that goal, remember baby steps are key. List those steps and note the ones you have completed. Be specific.

_____

_____

Gratitude List (10 mins). It's time to count your blessings!

_____

_____

Morning Workout (20 mins) Keep up the hard work! If you are pushing yourself, stick to it this week, don't give up now!

Walk or run, it doesn't matter, just move your body for 20 mins.

Yoga or other class you enjoy.

Gym: Did you push yourself in your workouts last week? Then keep it up this week. Hard work can change your body, energy level and confidence, so you can go kill that interview, land that new sales account or keep up with those busy kiddos. Repeat last week or chose a different sample workout created by a certified trainer on my website.

_____

_____

Morning Meal (10mins) If you have committed to removing processed food, even one or two items in your diet/at each meal and replaced them with real healthy food, I can imagine you are seeing a difference in not only your energy but maybe in those jeans too! Try not only eating a healthy breakfast and lunch but now try eating a healthy dinner too! It may take a little planning, but a little planning can go a long way and your family may thank you too! Check out my website for some good recipes for breakfast, lunch and dinner created by certified nutrition coach.

Track what you eat and how you feel.

_____

_____

Important Things to Do Today

_____

_____

WEEK TEN
DAY THREE

Date _____

Quiet Time (10mins) Chose 1 activity or find your own.
 Practice Breathing: Do breathing activity for 5 mins and try a meditation app for 5 mins, shake it up!
 Listen to a Meditation app: Abide app or app of choice.
 Pray, journal your prayers.
My own meditation activity today was, track any thoughts:

_____

_____

Goal Setting (10 mins) Continue to focus on that goal you set last week. I once heard a "goal is a dream with a deadline."
 Write down that goal each day this week. Continue to list the steps it takes to achieve that goal, remember baby steps are key. List those steps and note the ones you have completed. Be specific.

_____

_____

Gratitude List (10 mins). It's time to count your blessings!

_____

_____

Morning Workout (20 mins) Keep up the hard work! If you are pushing yourself, stick to it this week, don't give up now!

Walk or run, it doesn't matter, just move your body for 20 mins.

Yoga or other class you enjoy.

Gym: Did you push yourself in your workouts last week? Then keep it up this week. Hard work can change your body, energy level and confidence, so you can go kill that interview, land that new sales account or keep up with those busy kiddos. Repeat last week or chose a different sample workout created by a certified trainer on my website.

_____

_____

Morning Meal (10mins) If you have committed to removing processed food, even one or two items in your diet/at each meal and replaced them with real healthy food, I can imagine you are seeing a difference in not only your energy but maybe in those jeans too! Try not only eating a healthy breakfast and lunch but now try eating a healthy dinner too! It may take a little planning, but a little planning can go a long way and your family may thank you too! Check out my website for some good recipes for breakfast, lunch and dinner created by certified nutrition coach.

Track what you eat and how you feel.

_____

_____

Important Things to Do Today

_____

_____

WEEK TEN
DAY FOUR

Date _____

Quiet Time (10mins) Chose 1 activity or find your own.

Practice Breathing: Do breathing activity for 5 mins and try a meditation app for 5 mins, shake it up!

Listen to a Meditation app: Abide app or app of choice.

Pray, journal your prayers.

My own meditation activity today was, track any thoughts:

_____

_____

Goal Setting (10 mins) Continue to focus on that goal you set last week. I once heard a "goal is a dream with a deadline."

Write down that goal each day this week. Continue to list the steps it takes to achieve that goal, remember baby steps are key. List those steps and note the ones you have completed. Be specific.

_____

_____

Gratitude List (10 mins). It's time to count your blessings!

_____

_____

Morning Workout (20 mins) Keep up the hard work! If you are pushing yourself, stick to it this week, don't give up now!

      Walk or run, it doesn't matter, just move your body for 20 mins.

      Yoga or other class you enjoy.

      Gym: Did you push yourself in your workouts last week? Then keep it up this week. Hard work can change your body, energy level and confidence, so you can go kill that interview, land that new sales account or keep up with those busy kiddos. Repeat last week or chose a different sample workout created by a certified trainer on my website.

_____

_____

Morning Meal (10mins) If you have committed to removing processed food, even one or two items in your diet/at each meal and replaced them with real healthy food, I can imagine you are seeing a difference in not only your energy but maybe in those jeans too! Try not only eating a healthy breakfast and lunch but now try eating a healthy dinner too! It may take a little planning, but a little planning can go a long way and your family may thank you too! Check out my website for some good recipes for breakfast, lunch and dinner created by certified nutrition coach.

Track what you eat and how you feel.

_____

_____

Important Things to Do Today

_____

_____

WEEK TEN
DAY FIVE

Date _____

Quiet Time (10mins) Chose 1 activity or find your own.
     Practice Breathing: Do breathing activity for 5 mins and try a meditation app for 5 mins, shake it up!
     Listen to a Meditation app: Abide app or app of choice.
     Pray, journal your prayers.
My own meditation activity today was, track any thoughts:

_____

_____

Goal Setting (10 mins) Continue to focus on that goal you set last week. I once heard a "goal is a dream with a deadline."
     Write down that goal each day this week. Continue to list the steps it takes to achieve that goal, remember baby steps are key. List those steps and note the ones you have completed. Be specific.

_____

_____

Gratitude List (10 mins). It's time to count your blessings!

_____

_____

Morning Workout (20 mins) Keep up the hard work! If you are pushing yourself, stick to it this week, don't give up now!

Walk or run, it doesn't matter, just move your body for 20 mins.

Yoga or other class you enjoy.

Gym: Did you push yourself in your workouts last week? Then keep it up this week. Hard work can change your body, energy level and confidence, so you can go kill that interview, land that new sales account or keep up with those busy kiddos. Repeat last week or chose a different sample workout created by a certified trainer on my website.

_____

_____

Morning Meal (10mins) If you have committed to removing processed food, even one or two items in your diet/at each meal and replaced them with real healthy food, I can imagine you are seeing a difference in not only your energy but maybe in those jeans too! Try not only eating a healthy breakfast and lunch but now try eating a healthy dinner too! It may take a little planning, but a little planning can go a long way and your family may thank you too! Check out my website for some good recipes for breakfast, lunch and dinner created by certified nutrition coach.

Track what you eat and how you feel.

_____

_____

Important Things to Do Today

_____

_____

WEEK ELEVEN
DAY ONE

Date _____

Quiet Time (10mins) Chose 1 activity or find your own.

Practice Breathing: Do breathing activity for 5 mins and try a meditation app for 5 mins, shake it up!

Listen to a Meditation app: Abide app or app of choice.

Pray, and then **be still** and listen to what you hear.

My own meditation activity today was, track any thoughts:

_____

_____

Goal Setting (10 mins) Continue to focus on that goal, getting through the list of steps that you identified to get to that goal? If not, be real as to why, what are your roadblocks? Are those steps unrealistic, are you unsure of your ability to achieve them? Don't beat yourself up. We all do that - we are human, but keep trying! Remember consistency and hard work!

Continue to write down that goal each day this week. List the steps it takes to achieve that goal and if you are facing roadblocks, list the ways you may be able to overcome those hurdles. Be specific.

_____

_____

Gratitude List (10 mins). It's time to count your blessings!

_____

_____

Morning Workout (20mins) Keep up the hard work! If you are pushing yourself, stick to it this week, don't give up now!

Walk or run, it doesn't matter. Just move your body for 20 mins.

Yoga or other class you enjoy.

Gym: Did you push yourself in your workouts last week? Then keep it up this week. Hard work can change your body, energy level and confidence, so you can go kill that interview, land that new sales account or keep up with those busy kiddos. Repeat last week or chose a different sample workout created by a certified trainer on my website.

Morning Meal (10mins) If you have committed to removing processed food, even one or two items in your diet at each meal and replaced them with real healthy food, I can imagine you are seeing a difference in not only your energy but maybe in those jeans, too! Try not only eating a healthy breakfast and lunch, but now try eating a healthy dinner too! It may take a little planning, but a little planning can go a long way and your family may thank you too! Check out my website for some good recipes for breakfast, lunch and dinner created by certified nutrition coach.

Track what you eat and how you feel.

Important Things to Do Today

WEEK ELEVEN
DAY TWO

Date _____

Quiet Time (10mins) Chose 1 activity or find your own.

      Practice Breathing: Do breathing activity for 5 mins and try a meditation app for 5 mins, shake it up!

      Listen to a Meditation app: Abide app or app of choice.

      Pray, and then **be still** and listen to what you hear.

My own meditation activity today was, track any thoughts:

_____

_____

Goal Setting (10 mins) Continue to focus on that goal, getting through the list of steps that you identified to get to that goal? If not, be real as to why, what are your roadblocks? Are those steps unrealistic, are you unsure of your ability to achieve them? Don't beat yourself up. We all do that - we are human, but keep trying! Remember consistency and hard work!

      Continue to write down that goal each day this week. List the steps it takes to achieve that goal and if you are facing roadblocks, list the ways you may be able to overcome those hurdles. Be specific.

_____

_____

Gratitude List (10 mins). It's time to count your blessings!

_____

_____

215

Morning Workout (20mins) Keep up the hard work! If you are pushing yourself, stick to it this week, don't give up now!

Walk or run, it doesn't matter. Just move your body for 20 mins.

Yoga or other class you enjoy.

Gym: Did you push yourself in your workouts last week? Then keep it up this week. Hard work can change your body, energy level and confidence, so you can go kill that interview, land that new sales account or keep up with those busy kiddos. Repeat last week or chose a different sample workout created by a certified trainer on my website.

_____

_____

Morning Meal (10mins) If you have committed to removing processed food, even one or two items in your diet at each meal and replaced them with real healthy food, I can imagine you are seeing a difference in not only your energy but maybe in those jeans, too! Try not only eating a healthy breakfast and lunch, but now try eating a healthy dinner too! It may take a little planning, but a little planning can go a long way and your family may thank you too! Check out my website for some good recipes for breakfast, lunch and dinner created by certified nutrition coach.

Track what you eat and how you feel.

_____

_____

Important Things to Do Today

_____

_____

WEEK ELEVEN
DAY THREE

Date _____

Quiet Time (10mins) Chose 1 activity or find your own.

Practice Breathing: Do breathing activity for 5 mins and try a meditation app for 5 mins, shake it up!

Listen to a Meditation app: Abide app or app of choice.

Pray, and then **be still** and listen to what you hear.

My own meditation activity today was, track any thoughts:

_____

_____

Goal Setting (10 mins) Continue to focus on that goal, getting through the list of steps that you identified to get to that goal? If not, be real as to why, what are your roadblocks? Are those steps unrealistic, are you unsure of your ability to achieve them? Don't beat yourself up. We all do that - we are human, but keep trying! Remember consistency and hard work!

Continue to write down that goal each day this week. List the steps it takes to achieve that goal and if you are facing roadblocks, list the ways you may be able to overcome those hurdles. Be specific.

_____

_____

Gratitude List (10 mins). It's time to count your blessings!

_____

_____

Morning Workout (20mins) Keep up the hard work! If you are pushing yourself, stick to it this week, don't give up now!

Walk or run, it doesn't matter. Just move your body for 20 mins.

Yoga or other class you enjoy.

Gym: Did you push yourself in your workouts last week? Then keep it up this week. Hard work can change your body, energy level and confidence, so you can go kill that interview, land that new sales account or keep up with those busy kiddos. Repeat last week or chose a different sample workout created by a certified trainer on my website.

Morning Meal (10mins) If you have committed to removing processed food, even one or two items in your diet at each meal and replaced them with real healthy food, I can imagine you are seeing a difference in not only your energy but maybe in those jeans, too! Try not only eating a healthy breakfast and lunch, but now try eating a healthy dinner too! It may take a little planning, but a little planning can go a long way and your family may thank you too! Check out my website for some good recipes for breakfast, lunch and dinner created by certified nutrition coach.

Track what you eat and how you feel.

Important Things to Do Today

WEEK ELEVEN
DAY FOUR

Date _____

Quiet Time (10mins) Chose 1 activity or find your own.

Practice Breathing: Do breathing activity for 5 mins and try a meditation app for 5 mins, shake it up!

Listen to a Meditation app: Abide app or app of choice.

Pray, and then **be still** and listen to what you hear.

My own meditation activity today was, track any thoughts:

_____

_____

Goal Setting (10 mins) Continue to focus on that goal, getting through the list of steps that you identified to get to that goal? If not, be real as to why, what are your roadblocks? Are those steps unrealistic, are you unsure of your ability to achieve them? Don't beat yourself up. We all do that - we are human, but keep trying! Remember consistency and hard work!

Continue to write down that goal each day this week. List the steps it takes to achieve that goal and if you are facing roadblocks, list the ways you may be able to overcome those hurdles. Be specific.

_____

_____

Gratitude List (10 mins). It's time to count your blessings!

_____

_____

Morning Workout (20mins) Keep up the hard work! If you are pushing yourself, stick to it this week, don't give up now!

    Walk or run, it doesn't matter. Just move your body for 20 mins.

    Yoga or other class you enjoy.

    Gym: Did you push yourself in your workouts last week? Then keep it up this week. Hard work can change your body, energy level and confidence, so you can go kill that interview, land that new sales account or keep up with those busy kiddos. Repeat last week or chose a different sample workout created by a certified trainer on my website.

Morning Meal (10mins) If you have committed to removing processed food, even one or two items in your diet at each meal and replaced them with real healthy food, I can imagine you are seeing a difference in not only your energy but maybe in those jeans, too! Try not only eating a healthy breakfast and lunch, but now try eating a healthy dinner too! It may take a little planning, but a little planning can go a long way and your family may thank you too! Check out my website for some good recipes for breakfast, lunch and dinner created by certified nutrition coach.

    Track what you eat and how you feel.

Important Things to Do Today

WEEK ELEVEN
DAY FIVE

Date _____

Quiet Time (10mins) Chose 1 activity or find your own.
     Practice Breathing: Do breathing activity for 5 mins and try a meditation app for 5 mins, shake it up!
     Listen to a Meditation app: Abide app or app of choice.
     Pray, and then **be still** and listen to what you hear.

My own meditation activity today was, track any thoughts:

_____

_____

Goal Setting (10 mins) Continue to focus on that goal, getting through the list of steps that you identified to get to that goal? If not, be real as to why, what are your roadblocks? Are those steps unrealistic, are you unsure of your ability to achieve them? Don't beat yourself up. We all do that - we are human, but keep trying! Remember consistency and hard work!
     Continue to write down that goal each day this week. List the steps it takes to achieve that goal and if you are facing roadblocks, list the ways you may be able to overcome those hurdles. Be specific.

_____

_____

Gratitude List (10 mins). It's time to count your blessings!

_____

_____

227

Morning Workout (20mins) Keep up the hard work! If you are pushing yourself, stick to it this week, don't give up now!

      Walk or run, it doesn't matter. Just move your body for 20 mins.

      Yoga or other class you enjoy.

      Gym: Did you push yourself in your workouts last week? Then keep it up this week. Hard work can change your body, energy level and confidence, so you can go kill that interview, land that new sales account or keep up with those busy kiddos. Repeat last week or chose a different sample workout created by a certified trainer on my website.

_____

_____

Morning Meal (10mins) If you have committed to removing processed food, even one or two items in your diet at each meal and replaced them with real healthy food, I can imagine you are seeing a difference in not only your energy but maybe in those jeans, too! Try not only eating a healthy breakfast and lunch, but now try eating a healthy dinner too! It may take a little planning, but a little planning can go a long way and your family may thank you too! Check out my website for some good recipes for breakfast, lunch and dinner created by certified nutrition coach.

      Track what you eat and how you feel.

_____

_____

Important Things to Do Today

_____

_____

WEEK TWELVE
DAY ONE

YOU DID IT! BE PROUD, IF YOU COMMITTED TO BE OPEN MINDED AND JOURNAL CONSISTENTLY, YOU MOST LIKELY HAVE ACHIEVED MORE IN 3 MONTHS THAN MOST PEOPLE DO IN YEARS! CHANGE IS EMPOWERING! KEEP UP THE HARD WORK AND IF YOU HAVENT ALREADY DONE SO, ORDER YOUR NEXT 3 MONTH JOURNAL!
journalwaytosuccess.com

Date _____

Quiet Time (10mins) I hope you are feeling more peace throughout when you start day, remember these are activities you can do throughout the day as you face stress. Life is stressful so don't let it get the best of you! Chose 1 activity or find your own.

Practice Breathing: Do breathing activity for 5 mins and try a meditation app for 5 mins; shake it up!

Listen to a Meditation app: Abide app or app of choice.

Pray, and then **be still** and listen to what you hear.

My own meditation activity today was, track any thoughts:

_____

_____

Goal Setting (10 mins) Don't give up if you haven't achieved your goal you set out to accomplish. I know I can be so hard on myself if I don't do what I set my mind to do. I have learned to give myself some grace and be patient, I am not perfect but if I stay focused and work hard, I will figure it out! Maybe you want to focus on this goal for the next journal or maybe there is another goal you want to look at.

_____

_____

Gratitude List (10 mins). It's time to count your blessings!

_____

_____

Morning Workout (20mins) I am so proud of you; this can be so hard to do if you are not use to daily physical activity. Nice job! But understand balance is the key too. You need to listen to your body; there may be days you are not feeling it. That is the time to give yourself some grace. When I am feeling that, I may just take the day off or move to something less strenuous, but the key here is to not give up; practice, practice, practice!

Walk or run, it doesn't matter. Just move your body for 20 mins.

Yoga or other class you enjoy: I love to take a yoga class once or twice per week, along with a gym workout about 4 times per week; sometimes I just walk or take a hike with a friend.

Gym: Keep up the hard work, chose your favorite workouts this week.

Morning Meal (10mins) This is one of my most favorite activities. I LOVE food and I love seeing what a difference eating well makes in my life! I feel young and take no medication! Food is my medicine. People watch me eat healthy and they ask me how I do it. I laugh because they think for some reason, I don't have fun. Trust me, I enjoy meals out, I love wine and an amazing dessert. I just pace myself. I try to eat healthy all week and cheat on the weekends. But I also find I don't like cheating all weekend, because then I don't feel well and Monday stinks when I feel sluggish, bloated and tired. But if I am traveling or it is a special weekend, then it's all worth it. Again, it's all about balance. But don't give up. If you struggled here then try to focus on this section in your next journal. Remember, you are human, and you aren't perfect. All you can do is the best job you can. Regroup and in the next journal focus on this if you feel frustrated with your progress in this section.

Track what you eat and how you feel.

Important Things to Do Today

WEEK TWELVE
DAY TWO

Date _____

Quiet Time (10mins) I hope you are feeling more peace throughout when you start day, remember these are activities you can do throughout the day as you face stress. Life is stressful so don't let it get the best of you! Chose 1 activity or find your own.

Practice Breathing: Do breathing activity for 5 mins and try a meditation app for 5 mins; shake it up!

Listen to a Meditation app: Abide app or app of choice.

Pray, and then **be still** and listen to what you hear.

My own meditation activity today was, track any thoughts:

_____

_____

Goal Setting (10 mins) Don't give up if you haven't achieved your goal you set out to accomplish. I know I can be so hard on myself if I don't do what I set my mind to do. I have learned to give myself some grace and be patient, I am not perfect but if I stay focused and work hard, I will figure it out! Maybe you want to focus on this goal for the next journal or maybe there is another goal you want to look at.

_____

_____

Gratitude List (10 mins). It's time to count your blessings!

_____

_____

Morning Workout (20mins) I am so proud of you; this can be so hard to do if you are not use to daily physical activity. Nice job! But understand balance is the key too. You need to listen to your body; there may be days you are not feeling it. That is the time to give yourself some grace. When I am feeling that, I may just take the day off or move to something less strenuous, but the key here is to not give up; practice, practice, practice!

Walk or run, it doesn't matter. Just move your body for 20 mins.

Yoga or other class you enjoy: I love to take a yoga class once or twice per week, along with a gym workout about 4 times per week; sometimes I just walk or take a hike with a friend.

Gym: Keep up the hard work, chose your favorite workouts this week.

Morning Meal (10mins) This is one of my most favorite activities. I LOVE food and I love seeing what a difference eating well makes in my life! I feel young and take no medication! Food is my medicine. People watch me eat healthy and they ask me how I do it. I laugh because they think for some reason, I don't have fun. Trust me, I enjoy meals out, I love wine and an amazing dessert. I just pace myself. I try to eat healthy all week and cheat on the weekends. But I also find I don't like cheating all weekend, because then I don't feel well and Monday stinks when I feel sluggish, bloated and tired. But if I am traveling or it is a special weekend, then it's all worth it. Again, it's all about balance. But don't give up. If you struggled here then try to focus on this section in your next journal. Remember, you are human, and you aren't perfect. All you can do is the best job you can. Regroup and in the next journal focus on this if you feel frustrated with your progress in this section.

Track what you eat and how you feel.

Important Things to Do Today

WEEK TWELVE
DAY THREE

Date _____

Quiet Time (10mins) I hope you are feeling more peace throughout when you start day, remember these are activities you can do throughout the day as you face stress. Life is stressful so don't let it get the best of you! Chose 1 activity or find your own.

Practice Breathing: Do breathing activity for 5 mins and try a meditation app for 5 mins; shake it up!

Listen to a Meditation app: Abide app or app of choice.

Pray, and then **be still** and listen to what you hear.

My own meditation activity today was, track any thoughts:

_____

_____

Goal Setting (10 mins) Don't give up if you haven't achieved your goal you set out to accomplish. I know I can be so hard on myself if I don't do what I set my mind to do. I have learned to give myself some grace and be patient, I am not perfect but if I stay focused and work hard, I will figure it out! Maybe you want to focus on this goal for the next journal or maybe there is another goal you want to look at.

_____

_____

Gratitude List (10 mins). It's time to count your blessings!

_____

_____

Morning Workout (20mins) I am so proud of you; this can be so hard to do if you are not use to daily physical activity. Nice job! But understand balance is the key too. You need to listen to your body; there may be days you are not feeling it. That is the time to give yourself some grace. When I am feeling that, I may just take the day off or move to something less strenuous, but the key here is to not give up; practice, practice, practice!

Walk or run, it doesn't matter. Just move your body for 20 mins.

Yoga or other class you enjoy: I love to take a yoga class once or twice per week, along with a gym workout about 4 times per week; sometimes I just walk or take a hike with a friend.

Gym: Keep up the hard work, chose your favorite workouts this week.

_____

_____

Morning Meal (10mins) This is one of my most favorite activities. I LOVE food and I love seeing what a difference eating well makes in my life! I feel young and take no medication! Food is my medicine. People watch me eat healthy and they ask me how I do it. I laugh because they think for some reason, I don't have fun. Trust me, I enjoy meals out, I love wine and an amazing dessert. I just pace myself. I try to eat healthy all week and cheat on the weekends. But I also find I don't like cheating all weekend, because then I don't feel well and Monday stinks when I feel sluggish, bloated and tired. But if I am traveling or it is a special weekend, then it's all worth it. Again, it's all about balance. But don't give up. If you struggled here then try to focus on this section in your next journal. Remember, you are human, and you aren't perfect. All you can do is the best job you can. Regroup and in the next journal focus on this if you feel frustrated with your progress in this section.

Track what you eat and how you feel.

_____

_____

Important Things to Do Today

_____

_____

WEEK TWELVE
DAY FOUR

Date _____

Quiet Time (10mins) I hope you are feeling more peace throughout when you start day, remember these are activities you can do throughout the day as you face stress. Life is stressful so don't let it get the best of you! Chose 1 activity or find your own.

Practice Breathing: Do breathing activity for 5 mins and try a meditation app for 5 mins; shake it up!

Listen to a Meditation app: Abide app or app of choice.

Pray, and then **be still** and listen to what you hear.

My own meditation activity today was, track any thoughts:

_____

_____

Goal Setting (10 mins) Don't give up if you haven't achieved your goal you set out to accomplish. I know I can be so hard on myself if I don't do what I set my mind to do. I have learned to give myself some grace and be patient, I am not perfect but if I stay focused and work hard, I will figure it out! Maybe you want to focus on this goal for the next journal or maybe there is another goal you want to look at.

_____

_____

Gratitude List (10 mins). It's time to count your blessings!

_____

_____

Morning Workout (20mins) I am so proud of you; this can be so hard to do if you are not use to daily physical activity. Nice job! But understand balance is the key too. You need to listen to your body; there may be days you are not feeling it. That is the time to give yourself some grace. When I am feeling that, I may just take the day off or move to something less strenuous, but the key here is to not give up; practice, practice, practice!

Walk or run, it doesn't matter. Just move your body for 20 mins.

Yoga or other class you enjoy: I love to take a yoga class once or twice per week, along with a gym workout about 4 times per week; sometimes I just walk or take a hike with a friend.

Gym: Keep up the hard work, chose your favorite workouts this week.

Morning Meal (10mins) This is one of my most favorite activities. I LOVE food and I love seeing what a difference eating well makes in my life! I feel young and take no medication! Food is my medicine. People watch me eat healthy and they ask me how I do it. I laugh because they think for some reason, I don't have fun. Trust me, I enjoy meals out, I love wine and an amazing dessert. I just pace myself. I try to eat healthy all week and cheat on the weekends. But I also find I don't like cheating all weekend, because then I don't feel well and Monday stinks when I feel sluggish, bloated and tired. But if I am traveling or it is a special weekend, then it's all worth it. Again, it's all about balance. But don't give up. If you struggled here then try to focus on this section in your next journal. Remember, you are human, and you aren't perfect. All you can do is the best job you can. Regroup and in the next journal focus on this if you feel frustrated with your progress in this section.

Track what you eat and how you feel.

Important Things to Do Today

WEEK TWELVE
DAY FIVE

Date _____

Quiet Time (10mins) I hope you are feeling more peace throughout when you start day, remember these are activities you can do throughout the day as you face stress. Life is stressful so don't let it get the best of you! Chose 1 activity or find your own.

Practice Breathing: Do breathing activity for 5 mins and try a meditation app for 5 mins; shake it up!

Listen to a Meditation app: Abide app or app of choice.

Pray, and then **be still** and listen to what you hear.

My own meditation activity today was, track any thoughts:

_____

_____

Goal Setting (10 mins) Don't give up if you haven't achieved your goal you set out to accomplish. I know I can be so hard on myself if I don't do what I set my mind to do. I have learned to give myself some grace and be patient, I am not perfect but if I stay focused and work hard, I will figure it out! Maybe you want to focus on this goal for the next journal or maybe there is another goal you want to look at.

_____

_____

Gratitude List (10 mins). It's time to count your blessings!

_____

_____

Morning Workout (20mins) I am so proud of you; this can be so hard to do if you are not use to daily physical activity. Nice job! But understand balance is the key too. You need to listen to your body; there may be days you are not feeling it. That is the time to give yourself some grace. When I am feeling that, I may just take the day off or move to something less strenuous, but the key here is to not give up; practice, practice, practice!

Walk or run, it doesn't matter. Just move your body for 20 mins.

Yoga or other class you enjoy: I love to take a yoga class once or twice per week, along with a gym workout about 4 times per week; sometimes I just walk or take a hike with a friend.

Gym: Keep up the hard work, chose your favorite workouts this week.

_____

_____

Morning Meal (10mins) This is one of my most favorite activities. I LOVE food and I love seeing what a difference eating well makes in my life! I feel young and take no medication! Food is my medicine. People watch me eat healthy and they ask me how I do it. I laugh because they think for some reason, I don't have fun. Trust me, I enjoy meals out, I love wine and an amazing dessert. I just pace myself. I try to eat healthy all week and cheat on the weekends. But I also find I don't like cheating all weekend, because then I don't feel well and Monday stinks when I feel sluggish, bloated and tired. But if I am traveling or it is a special weekend, then it's all worth it. Again, it's all about balance. But don't give up. If you struggled here then try to focus on this section in your next journal. Remember, you are human, and you aren't perfect. All you can do is the best job you can. Regroup and in the next journal focus on this if you feel frustrated with your progress in this section.

Track what you eat and how you feel.

_____

_____

Important Things to Do Today

_____

_____

ABOUT THE AUTHOR

Sandie Troup grew up in Danville, California, where she was the oldest of three girls and is very close to her younger sisters, Linda and Jennifer. Sandie attended the University of Arizona in Tucson, where she received her bachelor's in Business Administration. After she married, she raised three kids, who went to the same high school as she did in Danville. Now her grown children Tyler (who is married to Alexa), Karley, and Lexy, and a granddaughter, Aria, all live in Colorado. Sandie loves to visit them often, and they all enjoy hiking, shopping, getting massages, and dining out together!

Sandie moved to Mesa, Arizona in 2017, where she began a new life after getting divorced after 33 years of marriage. Although Sandie lives in Arizona nine months out of the year, she spends summers in Colorado to avoid the heat of the Arizona summers.

In 30 years of experience as a Corporate Executive Recruiter and Career Coach, Sandie has helped global organizations manage complex recruitment programs and has hired thousands of qualified candidates. Seven years ago, she started her own business, where she focused primarily on headhunting and career coaching, but now she is redirecting her energy to the Career Coaching side of the business. Sandie recognized that the job search can be a great opportunity for a life transformation if you have the right tools to navigate it and that most struggle with those tools. Sandie's says, "In my program, we go above and beyond the frustrating online applications that recruiters don't read to building resumes, strong self-confidence, efficient networking ability, and powerful negotiation skills. The secret of success is rooted in one's beliefs about oneself, and the perfect time to shape it is at a young age."

Sandie offers professional guidance and support with the entire employment process. While maintaining her growing business, Sandie also supports an Environmental Health & Safety Consulting firm headquartered in the United Kingdom, where she supports their recruitment program for Professional Services in the West and Gulf Coast.

Sandie is passionate about her career but also passionate about her family and living a healthy, balanced life. She enjoys yoga, hiking, working out, reading and spends quality time with her family and friends.

Sandie is extremely involved in her local church where her faith has grown tremendously. She realizes that before she found her faith, she was lost and life never seemed to fall into place, because it was not built on a solid foundation. But now she has found that life is full of joy, passion, and unconditional love.

FOR MORE INFORMATION

Sandie Troup
Journal Your Way to Success
sandietroup12@gmail.com
journalwaytosuccess.com

Instagram sandietroup

Facebook sandietroup, Executive
Recruiter/Coach

Made in the USA
San Bernardino, CA
22 November 2019